Leading Schools and Sustaining Innovation

How can school leaders analyse and meaningfully engage in the complex process of change? Offering an innovative introduction to the challenges of school leadership from the perspective of systems, this essential staff-room companion shows why school leaders now need to think and engage as system leaders more than ever before.

Luke Roberts explores what types of systems can be most effectively implemented and provides cutting-edge ideas on what school leaders can do to embed and genuinely sustain innovation. He also presents a framework based on understanding different stakeholder views and shows how to facilitate process to gain new perspectives and enthuse the whole school community. This accessible resource focuses on the application, to enable readers to use their understanding of creativity and innovation to transform systems. He provides examples from research successfully conducted in schools as well as the lived experiences of working to change schools. He also helpfully provides a simple route to engaging with system thinking, asking what this means for the reader and the specific challenges they face.

Leading Schools and Sustaining Innovation will appeal to educationalists across the whole educational sector, including head teachers, policy leaders as well as staff working towards and passionate about school improvement and transformation.

Luke Roberts has worked in Education for more than 20 years helping school communities and leaders to change their systems. He is passionate about the power of education to change lives and inspire creativity to address complex challenges.

Leading Schools and Sustaining Innovation

How to Think Big and Differently in Complex Systems

Luke Roberts

LONDON AND NEW YORK

Designed cover image: Credit goes to Scriberia for the cover image of the book

First published 2024
by Routledge
4 Park Square, Milton Park, Abingdon, Oxon OX14 4RN

and by Routledge
605 Third Avenue, New York, NY 10158

Routledge is an imprint of the Taylor & Francis Group, an informa business

© 2024 Luke Roberts

The right of Luke Roberts to be identified as author of this work has been asserted in accordance with sections 77 and 78 of the Copyright, Designs and Patents Act 1988.

All rights reserved. No part of this book may be reprinted or reproduced or utilised in any form or by any electronic, mechanical, or other means, now known or hereafter invented, including photocopying and recording, or in any information storage or retrieval system, without permission in writing from the publishers.

Trademark notice: Product or corporate names may be trademarks or registered trademarks, and are used only for identification and explanation without intent to infringe.

British Library Cataloguing-in-Publication Data
A catalogue record for this book is available from the British Library

Library of Congress Cataloging-in-Publication Data
Names: Roberts, Luke, 1976- author.
Title: Leading schools and sustaining innovation : how to think big and differently in complex systems / Luke Roberts.
Description: Abingdon, Oxon ; New York, NY : Routledge, 2024. | Includes bibliographical references and index.
Identifiers: LCCN 2023014207 | ISBN 9781032015613 (hardback) | ISBN 9781032015620 (paperback) | ISBN 9781003179108 (ebook)
Subjects: LCSH: Educational leadership. | Educational change. | System theory.
Classification: LCC LB2806 .R5688 2024 | DDC 371.2/011--dc23/eng/20230614
LC record available at https://lccn.loc.gov/2023014207

ISBN: 978-1-032-01561-3 (hbk)
ISBN: 978-1-032-01562-0 (pbk)
ISBN: 978-1-003-17910-8 (ebk)

DOI: 10.4324/9781003179108

Typeset in Galliard
by SPi Technologies India Pvt Ltd (Straive)

For:
Jasmine and Alexander

Contents

Acknowledgements ix

1 Why think of schools as systems? 1
2 Getting to know systems 10
3 Complex adaptive systems 26
4 Energy in schools 46
5 Understanding your system 61
6 Systems leaders 78
7 Leading system change 94
8 Sustaining systems change in educational settings 112
9 Conclusions on thinking big and thinking differently 132

References *139*
Index *142*

Acknowledgements

This book could not be possible without the many wonderful, stimulating and challenging conversations I have had with so many people it is not possible to name them all here but shows the beauty of an interconnected world. I would also like to thank my family for their generosity of time to allow me to put my thoughts on paper and complete this book. Finally, I would like to thank my nonagenarian gran Winifred Amabile, who has been a constant support and fountain of advice and encouragement throughout the creation of this book. She is a system thinker beyond her time, and I am deeply grateful.

I am grateful to Scriberia for granting permissions to use all their designed artwork in *Leading Schools and Sustaining Innovation*. The credit for all the visuals in this book goes to Scriberia.

1 Why think of schools as systems?

1.1 Introduction

Welcome to a book about schools as systems. This book aims to be a useful guide to thinking about school change. It will present questions through the lens of schools and other educational settings as a system. This lens of schools as systems will seek to explain why organisational change in educational settings can be challenging for leaders. Furthermore, when leaders do successfully implement change, the issue of sustaining educational benefits is difficult to do. This book will introduce readers to a complexity approach. So let me reassure you now that you don't need to have a background in System Thinking or Complexity Theory; there is already a wide literature on these topics. Rather, you will be introduced to some of these ideas but in a way that makes them accessible and relatable to the context of schools, and hopefully your own setting. For those interested in a deeper understanding, there will be references along the way. However, my main goal is to show through my experiences and research how these ideas can be applied to schools. In doing so, I hope this allows you to make links with your experiences and challenges and the systems you wish to change. Before we explore these ideas, let me share some of my background so you have a better understanding of why me and why now?

1.1.1 My academic journey

One of my earliest school memories is seeing a comment in my primary school report saying, "Luke has a happy-go-lucky attitude", and thinking how lovely it was to be described as happy *and* lucky. However, looking back, I see that I never fully engaged in my London-based primary and secondary education. I invariably felt that I didn't quite 'get it', as I was striving to understand how things fit together and decipher a pattern that would make sense of it all.

Only after my mum took a secondary-school teaching job in Hong Kong and I started my A-levels that I began to recognise how highly teachers valued education, how passionately they cared about their topics and how much my fellow pupils admired educational success. This marked a turning point, when

DOI: 10.4324/9781003179108-1

I realised for the first time that some people pursued educational aspirations beyond simply achieving the task set in the classroom. For me to see teachers who wanted to debate, inspire and ultimately put students on a path to the future was so different from what I had experienced in London.

After succeeding in my A-levels, I studied Law and Politics at university. However, I struggled with the writing volumes in exams and often ran out of time, frequently resorting to a hastily drawn mind map to show what I *would* have written. I also had difficulties grasping legal terminology's Latin words and spellings. Nevertheless, I liked phrases such as *tempus fugit* and *carpe diem* and enjoyed the logical debates and arguments intrinsic to Law, particularly questions of definition, how lawyers could argue so fiercely over the meaning of a word.

Nonetheless, my academic challenges took their toll. After graduating in 2001, I fell out of love with learning until my future wife encouraged me to begin a part-time Open University MBA six years later, in which I focused on creativity and innovation in schools. I had just been asked to chair a pilot project across four London councils to reduce exclusions. My academic studies helped me see the practical meaning and everyday relevance of business concepts in my working life at Lambeth Local Education Authority, exploring their functional significance and application. I remember sitting in a Local Authority meeting soon after learning about the concept of 'groupthink' in the MBA course, watching the meeting members agree on a course of action without any critical discussion of the potential implications (or representation for the community) and realising that I was witnessing 'groupthink' in action. It was very exciting to see theory in practice.

Studying while still working helped me bridge the gap between theory and practice, meaning I always considered academic concepts through a practical 'work' lens. Drawn to the idea of 'concepts in action' and how system ideas look when applied to complex, tangled issues in the real world of school communities. I began to question the prevailing theory of school change which I had promoted in the Local Authority role. I shared my observations and concerns about achieving school change using the Whole School Approach as a keynote speaker at a restorative practice conference in 2010, challenging the predominant thinking at the time, which was based focusing on the benefits rather than the challenges of implementation I had seen. Though this prompted a degree of professional discord among some attendees, Professor Hilary Cremin – then Dr Cremin – approached me afterwards to suggest I begin validating my critique. "Since you have no evidence to back up what you are saying," she asked me, "would you like to come to Cambridge to find it?" I replied with an enthusiastic "Yes!"

I thus embarked in 2012 on my Educational Research master's on the Myth of Whole School Approach, seeking to validate the Whole School Approach (WSA). While 'school change' relates to the action taken and its outcome (this may be intentional or unintentional), the Whole School Approach describes the nature of a *process*, which predominately focuses on senior leaders' buy-in;

teachers, staff, being trained; and a policy created to effect school change. Over time it has evolved to include other aspects such as students and parents/carers, and forms of performance data. However, my master's research identified from the existing literature on various studies that there was scant evidence for the WSA's success. My findings showed that, at best, WSA helps educational leaders think through aspects of implementation. At worst, it disempowers leaders through prescriptive efforts to effect educational change, minimises local context, and marginalises school community voices. In effect, the WSA fails to do what it says, but is common currency for the next educational fashion to gain credence by insisting on this as the change model.

These findings prompted me to seek concepts-in-action that resonate with the reality of systems change in schools. To this end, I began a PhD late in 2013 to explore (*a*) what happens beyond the excitement of implementation and (*b*) the factors facilitating sustainable change in schools. This equipped me with a much deeper understanding of why theories for leading and sustaining innovation in schools have not kept up with leaders' needs on the ground, as this book will show.

However, I found the first year of my PhD painful and difficult, constantly feeling that I didn't 'get it' and that my lifetime's accumulation of coping strategies fell short of the PhD's requirements. Just as I was on the cusp of quitting at the beginning of my second year, Professor Cremin suggested I get tested for dyslexia. To my great surprise, I was diagnosed with both dyslexia and dyspraxia. Though unexpected, the diagnosis made sense of the dissonance I'd experienced in my academic journey and the ever-present feeling that I did not understand or apply things the way the system expected me to. This, I had 'lived' experience of the reality of being neurodiverse in systems which did not recognise multiple ways of learning. Rather, than feeling disconnected from learning, I now had a framework for understanding the strengths of being neurodiverse. While there is no one 'right' way of thinking, learning, and responding, mine had never seemed to 'fit' the educational system's blueprint. This was in part because rather than seeking to 'deconstruct' problems, I wanted to explore and find connection. However, I began realising the flip side: that the education system fails to recognise diversity in how different people can perceive, experience and interact with the same system.

1.1.1.1 Professional engagement with the English educational system

I began working with the English educational system as soon as I graduated, and was fortunate to be employed by Dame Jocelyn Barrow (DBE)[1] and Dawn Hill (CBE) on a consultation to gauge the local appetite for a new form of school organisation (later to become Lambeth Academy). At the time, it was potentially the country's first to be run by a Trust rather than a Local Authority. The consultation also spanned a unique socio-cultural mix, engaging with one of London's most deprived communities (the Notre Dame estate) and one of its most affluent, Clapham Common communities (where property sold for well over £1 million). The community's diversity of educational perspectives and aspirations gave me invaluable insight and appreciation of the complex needs and expectations schools can face.

My next job at a research company involved conducting interviews and issuing surveys about bullying in 36 schools across England and Wales, building my experience engaging directly with students, staff and leaders. Experiencing so many schools across such diverse locations also highlighted the vast spectrum of school cultures, ranging from those affected by the high levels of transitory workers in Blackpool, to Scunthorpe, where multiple generations of the same family were taught by the same teacher. I vividly remember the ever-present smell of the cheese factory down the road when working in large secondary school in Oxfordshire, and the teachers' frustration that, because so many local people would end up employed there, the local community did not see the wider need for education.

Struck by the diversity of school experiences, I devised a simple test. What do you feel a new visitor would see in the first two minutes in a school's reception area? I would base my answer on a few simple questions: What was on the walls? How was I greeted? Was I even acknowledged? Did pupils and staff say 'hello'? All of these things give a first impression of what the school culture is like, but become missed in the daily rituals and routines of school life. I also noticed that a school's architecture reflected the prevailing ideas when it was built (e.g., the 1960s comprehensive or 1980s Brutalism). I also remember thinking how bizarre some school designs were, ranging from warrens of long, narrow corridors to bunker-like buildings in the middle of housing estates. Sometimes it felt like architects don't actually seem to want to link the design to the humans inside and how the building can actually affect the culture of the community inside.

Moving on from the research company in 2005, I became one of the first local authority coordinators for restorative practice, this time working in Lambeth's local authority in London. Armed on my first day with a wealth of evidence for restorative practice, I remember visiting a secondary school to meet the deputy head, where I sat and explained to her how she could successfully implement restorative practice to address bullying in the school. As I walked across the playground afterwards, my new boss Mick called me. "What do you think you did wrong in that meeting?" he asked. My mind racing, I realised I had failed to listen to the Deputy Head or empathise with where she was and what her needs were and acknowledged my mistake to Mick. "Good", he responded, "I'll arrange a meeting next week where you can discuss again what you could do with the school". Such experiences taught me that working with school leaders was a balancing act between acknowledging their unique experiences and needs and identifying how change could support their future vision of the school.

Lambeth's substantial deprivation levels, multicultural tensions, and community needs also broadened my understanding and awareness of the issues school leaders face. Such issues presented considerable challenges in engaging children and young people, negotiating the enduring legacy of racism in some parts of the community, and dealing with the discrimination against (at the time) the new Polish community that emerged from the backlash against European immigration.

After applying and refining restorative approaches in Lambeth, I then moved to Croydon Council in 2008, where I gained invaluable experience working with London's largest youth population. Deepening my knowledge and experience further by working with other boroughs across London and England, I eventually set up my own consultancy in 2010 to champion restorative practices' role in addressing ingrained educational issues ranging from exclusion to school culture.

1.1.1.2 Recognising the gap between theory and practice in schools

I had experienced great success working with schools and creating school networks supporting innovation ... or so I thought. Having set up a highly successful secondary school and primary school network in Lambeth, a secondary-school behaviour mentor I'd worked closely with and greatly respected called me about two years later, inviting me back to provide staff training. This struck me as strange; I thought I had left a vibrant network of schools with enthusiastic and highly trained staff. Moreover, the data showed a reduction in exclusions and increases in student engagement. "Job done", I thought. So why was I being contacted?

The simple answer is that the school network had collapsed over time. Because the local authority did not replace my role, efforts to sustain the network gradually declined as other school priorities took precedence. Still, I had diligently followed national guidance, delivered local authority outcomes, secured senior-leadership buy-in across the schools, changed school policies and increased staff awareness through training, so the collapse was surprising. What was going on?

To answer this, I began questioning the Whole School Approach in my Master's on Educational Research,[2] conducting interviews with staff to explore their experience of implementation. My initial findings indicated leaders considered the process complete once staff received training, assuming they had provided all the expertise and knowledge staff needed to effect organisational change. Having worked with all school types, however, I knew how critical it was to engage staff and understand their experiences. Sure enough, once I began interviewing them, it became clear that there was a lack of post-training follow-up and support.

I began wondering why some schools implemented and retained such training while, in others, it drained away like bathwater. I was fortunate to discuss this with Professor Tony Booth, one of the writers of the "Index for Inclusion". His work guides schools' development of learning and participation but focuses on the key purpose of schools which is to educate. He encouraged me to consider a *school's* fundamental purpose (distinct from government policy), explaining that because schools are an eco-system geared towards one primary goal, any attempt to innovate or change the system will always be secondary. Therefore, the WSA would always fail as the change was not linked to the primary purpose. His insight shook the foundations of my understanding and prompted a complete paradigm shift. "Wow", I thought, "I've been looking at everything through entirely the wrong lens". Though his words challenged the core of my professional ideology and left me deeply concerned that my good intentions had been misguided about school change. Tony Booth was kind enough to help me reconfigure my axiological[3] conceptualisation. I realised I needed a new way to think about school change that recognised school leaders' on-the-ground issues and challenges. In short, I'd identified the problem but did not know the answer.

1.2 Considering a new approach: why now?

Education's challenge is to retain what already works while continuously finding ways towards greater alignment with the needs of children, young people, parents and their communities. However, the nature of the communities schools serve has changed dramatically, with developments in social media and technology competing for young people's attention in new ways. Schools are facing concerns about staff as well as students' mental health greater than ever before. Although online social platforms promise an expanded global perspective, for example, their algorithm-based feeds often create echo-chambers instead, giving the false impression that other people think the same way we do. The changes in society often influence schools first, which means that school leaders are often faced with innovating solutions that parents and governments have yet to address.

In addition, England's educational marketisation means education providers must compete and collaborate in unprecedented ways – all while dealing with educational regulators' demands for new data and information about their activities. Lastly, it is unclear whether school leadership – and School Leadership Theory – has kept up with these changes.

Educational leaders must negotiate these issues daily and constantly adapt to new challenges and developments, usually with mixed results. However, tempting it is to blame individuals and conclude that leadership is not up to the job, this is not the whole story. Instead, this book argues that educational leadership now needs to think big and think differently about the challenges schools face.

1.3 Understanding the bigger picture

I often see senior leadership teams' unwittingly perpetuate the daily problems they face – not because they don't have the energy or passion for addressing them, but because they lack the right analytical tools to understand what their underlying forces and dynamics are. Approaches such as the WSA oversimplify the complex, messy and interconnected matrix of variables moderating school change, underestimating the systemic barriers of the very change they wish to bring about. As a result, school communities' enthusiasm for new but narrowly conceived initiatives is often short-lived.

The best school leaders I have worked with intuitively grasped their school system's complexity while maintaining a clear vision for its future. While others have tried to use their power or personality to control, bully or charm their way through difficult situations, this all has varying degrees of success, but ultimately fails. In this book, I argue that there is an urgent need for school leaders to become system-aware, avoiding the seduction of simplicity. Hence, schools seeking to sustain innovation within their complex existing systems must think big and differently.

1.4 Systems in action

When introducing thinking in systems to a new audience, I am usually asked two questions: (*a*) "Why is this useful?" and (*b*) "How can I apply this to my specific situation?". This book aims to answer the first by helping the reader understand and clarify the type of system they are in and their aspirations for changing it. Because 'systems change' is a broad term covering a range of system types, systems leaders must understand their system's identity, the utility and benefits and challenges of change in educational settings. As I will explain in Chapters 2 and 3, different types of systems require different skills to enact lasting change. Knowing the difference is essential for schools leaders to avoid pitfalls which build resent and fatigue in their schools communities.

Answering the second question requires the correct analytical framework for understanding desired change versus *required* change. For example, a UK school that has scored poorly in its school inspection may naturally want to progress from a "requires improvement" rating to a "good" one. However, broader social-organisation issues such as culture, relationships and power dynamics often hinder leaders' intentions. Change cannot be superimposed onto the existing social system; instead, the current system must be understood and modified to elicit the desired change. Recognition of your specific system requires the reader to be system-curious, rather than seeking 'quick wins', the 'low-hanging fruit' or whatever clichéd phrase for short-term gains you would like to add.

This book aims to help school leaders avoid the compelling trap of 'activity'. The temptation to take action and be seen *doing something* underlies the seductiveness of school efficiency/effectiveness maxims for school leaders. However, thinking in systems requires leaders to consider changes within the school's complex relationship web. While school efficiency and effectiveness promise improvement according to a hidden set of pre-defined assumptions, this book argues that achieving a change, transformation or metamorphosis depends on understanding a school's unique system to create and sustain changes which benefit its social eco-system.

I believe this approach offers a cornucopia of potential benefits. First, an increased system awareness will enable school leaders to make decisions that deliver genuine and authentic change. Second, as leaders understand how to craft their school system's capability, they will be better placed to tackle issues neglected in the 'too difficult' pile or addressed in a hurry (out of a desire for immediate action) in a more nuanced, holistic and sustainable way.

By the end of this book, I hope the reader will be able to confidently describe (*a*) the challenges of engaging with systems and (*b*) how to effect positive, sustainable changes to achieve long-term impacts in their setting.

1.5 Self-reflection: recognising our position in the system

It is easy to assume that 'leadership' references the person or people at the top of the organisational hierarchy, who thus lead the system. However, it is vital to recognise how different this view can be depending on where you are in the system, and how important such alternative perspectives are in identifying what to do and how to do it. Among other benefits, I hope this book will enable readers to reflect on what the 'thinking' means to them regardless of how others identify their positions in the system.

It is equally important to recognise *what* the leaders seek to change. While this sounds self-evident, identifying the types of power that are influencing and being influenced by system decision-making is essential. Schools, like all forms of social systems, have power in them, and how to work with and round such issues will be essential.

Moreover, since today's actions will influence future requirements, system-energy is another critical aspect of the craft of thinking in systems. However, many leadership approaches fail to consider how systems leaders energize themselves for the change to come. To become a reflective system leader, school leaders must practice self-awareness by reflecting on where they are in in terms of the ebbs and flows of the school. As one head teacher said, "I always employ people who are smarter than me" (though I suspect this was a half-truth, as he was aware enough to *know* that they were smarter than him and understand how to manage them). Being reflective of what and when you are doing things is essential to engaging with your own and the wider energy in the system.

Self-awareness in systems is more than role-modelling a particular managerial style or value. It also includes questions of influence, unintended consequences, empathy and decision-making, especially in crisis situations. If thinking big and thinking differently is required, then reflecting on where you are and why you do what you do matters. While many change-management approaches assume the agent of change is somehow separate from the change itself, reflective practice in systems involves recognising that you, too, are part of the system; it influences you, and you influence it. By definition, a systems leader must consider the interdependencies and interconnection you – yes, you, dear reader – are part of. This book offers a range of reflective questions, developed through professional experience and academic research, to help you. Instead of trying to provide a one-size-fits-all toolkit, it offers a new lens for looking at the educational world.

1.6 Chapter overviews

Chapter 2, "Getting to know systems", briefly reviews the historical roots of today's organisational management approaches before introducing various system types, including simple, complicated and chaotic systems. It provides general examples of each, followed by specific school-based examples.

Chapter 3, "Complex adaptive systems", introduces a framework for understanding complex adaptive systems that focuses on amplification and feedback, self-organisation, emergence, boundaries and time.

Chapter 4, "Energy in schools", explores how a system's social energy can generate change or maintain the status quo.

Chapter 5, "Understanding your system", demonstrates different ways of defining and describing a system, helping system leaders to develop and share mental models with other stakeholders.

Chapter 6, "System leaders", explores what it means to be a leader in a complex adaptive system and how this requires a new mindset for engaging with complexity and emergence in schools.

Chapter 7, "Leading system change", applies the previous chapters learning to a school setting, outlining what can be done to shift a school (or a network of schools) into a new system state.

Chapter 8: "Sustaining system change", moves beyond the world of implementation and what system leaders need to do to sustain the success they have in changing their school or system.

Chapter 9: "Conclusions to thinking big and thinking differently", will offer reflections on key insights along the way and what thinking systems have to offer to enable leaders to truly think big and differently.

The preliminaries have now been covered; you know why me and why now; let's begin to together to understand why we need to think of schools as systems and why this matters to enable you, my reader, to think big and differently.

Notes

1 Dame Jocelyn Barrow, 15 April 1929–9 April 2020, was an educational pioneer and campaigned for the Race Relations Act, 1976.
2 2010–2013 at Cambridge University.
3 A philosophical theory of values, moral or aesthetic.

2 Getting to know systems

2.1 We need to change the system!

We often hear cries of "we need to change the system" for various issues, be it climate change, online child protection or, in this book's case, educational change. When calling for system change, most people mean wholesale change across the entire system. Instead, I ask, "*Which* system do you want to change?" Since some systems are easier to change than others, this distinction is critical; we must get to know the system we want to change.

System thinking requires a different mindset from forms of conventional leadership. Like many organisational-management types, school management has been susceptible to 'component thinking'. Hence, leadership theories generally encourage school leaders to improve the school's individual components (e.g., teaching, pedagogy, policy or finance), reasoning that improving the constituent parts will improve the whole system. As we shall see this form of 'component thinking' is widespread to the point it now often goes unchallenged, yet it is important to recognise the history of how this way of thinking became dominant in educational leaders minds?

2.2 The legacy of component thinking

Component thinking originates in Taylorism, named after the American engineer Frederick Winslow Taylor (1856–1915). A passionate advocate of efficiency and effectiveness on the factory floor, Taylor developed his theory of the scientific organisation of work in the midst of American Industrialisation, publishing his ideas in his 1911 book, *The Principles of Scientific Management*. He sought to improve factory efficiency by breaking down every job into its simplest repetitive component tasks, enabling unskilled labourers to complete them as efficiently as possible. He thus aimed to replace artisans or craftspeople, who could only produce a single skilfully crafted unique item at a time.

For Taylor, workers were not there to think or create but to execute clear, pre-defined tasks in tightly controlled ways. As his book declared,

> Now one of the very first requirements for a man who is fit to handle pig iron as a regular occupation is that he shall be so stupid and so

phlegmatic that he more nearly resembles in his mental make-up the ox than any other type.

(1911, p. 59)

It is tempting to judge Taylor by our own standards, but even in his own time he had a contempt for workers for whom he was developing his scientific (great bit of marketing to call this scientific) method. He thus believed that "every single act of every workman can be reduced to a science" (1911, p. 64). Taylor's 'scientific method' was, therefore, to reduce tasks to their most basic constituent parts for the workforce – the assembly line – and increase their efficiency via faster completion of their specific task. Taylorism still underlies many leadership theories which continue emphasis on improvement through efficiency and effectiveness, including educational leadership.

One enduring consequence of Taylorism is some organisational management's dehumanising effect on working experience, especially in schools. Although management theory has gradually discarded Taylor's explicit contemptuous attitude towards the workforce, his theory's dehumanising legacy remains. This is evident in the all-too common "management knows best" rhetoric, which considers workers too "stupid and phlegmatic" to understand the bigger picture. Indeed, many organisations, particularly schools, adhere to Taylorism principles without being aware that these originated in a different industrial era. Nevertheless, Taylor's ideas are so powerful that they continue to shape expectations of what 'successful leadership' means in education, and therefore they go unchallenged.

This 'efficiency and effectiveness' drive has influenced many sectors, including not-for-profit and educational agendas. Many countries thus use some form of inspection framework to ensure the quality of their educational provision and standards. Educational policies have sought to raise educational achievement through ever-increasing pressure on schools to be more efficient in raising standards. School leaders have also been influenced by a Taylor-based perception of how to run schools on being efficient and effective. Thus, the legacy of Taylorism has survived in school leadership theory.

2.2.1 Education as a societal production line

Hence, we can take the lens of the educational system as a giant machine through which society seeks to produce standardised education levels as effectively and efficiently as possible. Using the educational production-line metaphor, the school expects children to pass through various component stages that input learning via teaching, transforming them into qualified workers capable of following instructions. Here, the idea of a workforce ready for an industrial society means that the production line can disregard 'defective' children, that is, children who do not meet the standards required to move through the production line to become work-ready or able to pass exams to the benefit of the school's results.

However, viewing the educational system as a production line has several consequences. First, it defines efficiency as effectiveness, requiring constant pressure to maximise the core function: educational exam results. Efficiency thus determines leaders' decisions on students' movements, time spent on particular subjects, training provision for staff and cost of extracurricular activities. Furthermore, production-line management theory uses performance targets to compare efficiencies. Hence, in England there are school League Tables. 'Standards' as a form of minimum quality control and 'learning objectives' are used to ensure all students receive identical 'inputs' along the production line. This leaves little opportunity for creativity as this creates variance which undermines 'standards' in teaching because ultimately the production line does not trust individuals.

In addition, pressures to be ever-more effective drive leaders and educationalists' endless search for techniques, strategies and 'quick-wins' to maintain and enhance efficiency. As a consequence, school leaders can end up constantly seeking new fads which are the equivalent to production-line 'cogs' (educational trends) promising to increase the machine's efficiency and effectiveness. I have often wondered how easily un-evidenced fads can get into the minds of educational leaders, yet highly evidenced initiatives often fail. Thus, as school leaders master this form of management, education's fundamental purpose gradually erodes. For teachers, workloads increase, staff burnout accelerates, staff retention declines, presenteeism and absenteeism increase and recruitment becomes more challenging – who would want to join an educational production line? For students, exclusion levels rise – especially for marginalized groups producing less desirable results – and the curriculum-driven learning experience bypasses topic exploration in favour of passing assessments. As a result, the production line's 'outputs' are what success can be viewed as rather than the student's experience. Therefore, schools following a production-line approach ultimately show a disconnect between the meaning of education and the results-oriented outcomes of exams. However, rather than taking the simplistic view that it is school leaders' fault, I argue the adherence to Taylorist management theory (in the guise of Educational Leadership Theory) is to blame.

In the English educational system (the one I am most familiar with), the production-line approach is most pervasive in the state or public sector, which has reinforced educational pressure to perform via an artificial market model that creates the illusion of parent choice. This model drives schools to become ever-more efficient, under the core argument of raising educational standards. The Office for Standards in Education, Children's Services and Skills (Ofsted) evaluates schools against four criteria:

- The quality of education
- Behaviour and attitudes
- Personal development
- Leadership and management

Schools are judged on each criterion according to a set of descriptors, assessed via evidence gathered by Ofsted inspectors. The results determine the school's classification into one of four Ofsted categories: 'Outstanding', 'Good', 'Requires improvement' and 'Inadequate'. To be rated as 'Outstanding', a school must achieve this standard across all four criteria. Ofsted then judges the school's overall effectiveness according to outcomes of the educational systems purpose: to prepare students to successfully achieve educational qualifications, for example, GCSEs and A-Levels, equipping them for university. Therefore, the educational production line's function is to achieve this as efficiently and effectively as possible. In effect, Ofsted provides quality assurance for an educational system based on a management theory that is over 100 years out of date – a testament to its remarkably enduring influence.

This book argues that education is not best served by a management theory developed for the industrial-era's organisational principles. Moreover, Taylor's ideas risk dehumanising the workforce by reducing educationalists to unskilled production-line workers rather than experts crafting the future. In its relentless pursuit of greater efficiency and effectiveness, the education system prioritises outcome-based indicators of educational success, that is, exam-based targets and performance measures, to the detriment of both staff and students.

2.2.2 Quantifying outputs: League Tables

In England and Wales, the introduction of League Tables in 1993 reflected this rise in exam-based targets and performance measures. Policymakers reasoned that public access to schools' performance indicators would enable parents to make more informed decisions about which school to send their children to.

League Table rankings depend on several performance measures. The first is the Standard Assessment Test (SAT), introduced in 1988. Children sit these exams in the final year of primary school, aged 10–11. These are followed by GCSEs (General Certificate of Education), introduced in 1986, and A-Levels (Advanced Level qualification), established in 1951. However, it is beyond this book's scope to debate their purpose, relative merit and cumulative influence on teaching and learning processes. Instead, our focus is on the comparative yardstick they represent, enabling schools to assess their performance against other schools and ultimately becoming the focal point for defining, operationalising and measuring educational improvement. In this sense, League Tables rank schools according to their efficiency and effectiveness in achieving exam-based outcomes. Thus, they make perfect sense for a production-line approach, comparing the different outputs of distinct educational conveyor belts: SATs, GCSEs and A-levels.

League Tables changed the focus of education in several ways. Firstly, they led to over-subscription in some schools and under-subscription in others by generating differential parental demand and preference. Parents who can afford to buy or rent in a particular school catchment area can choose a better-performing school for their children. This creates what Donella Meadow terms "success to the successful", rewarding the League Table 'winners' with the means to score highly again while making it difficult for low-achieving schools serving some of the most deprived communities in the country to move up the League Table. Hence, rather than showing performance, it can be argued that League Tables simply reflect the dominant influence of affluence in education, inadvertently widening performance gaps between schools. Moreover, League Tables rely on performance targets that reduce the context, skill and joy of learning, oversimplifying a complex process.

Secondly, League Tables encourage school leaders to seek status in the rankings rather than the relationships with the community. While working in Local Authority many years ago, I learned that a head teacher had hired a local community centre to relocate disruptive pupils during an Ofsted inspection, ensuring that the inspectors would see only well-behaved classes. As a result, Ofsted judged the school to be efficient and effective. In this case, the pressure of the Ofsted inspection led the head teacher to prioritise status over the community, physically removing difficult students rather than supporting them. Indeed, as schools leaders have sought greater status, more punitive behaviour-management systems have emerged to reduce the time teachers spend on disruptive behaviour. Such systems use rewards and sanctions to regulate acceptable norms in the conveyer belt's operations of schools. Examples include isolation rooms (referred to as 'internal exclusion'), where children and young people are forbidden from talking to anyone,[1] and external fixed-term exclusion, which can last up to 45 days. Finally, schools can resort to permanent exclusion, removing a child from the school entirely. The key point here is that although disruptive behaviour may have always been an issue in schools, an unintended consequence of League Tables has been to reduce inclusivity as school leaders seek to acquire or maintain status in their rankings, both for the school and themselves.

Although Ofsted considers a school's exclusion figures when assessing effectiveness, schools have evolved an 'off-rolling' strategy to get around this. There is no formal definition, but Ofsted states that

> [o]ff-rolling is the practice of removing a pupil from the school roll without using a permanent exclusion, when removal is primarily in the best interests of the school, rather than the best interests of the pupil. This includes pressuring a parent to remove their child from the school roll.[2]

As well as minimising exclusion figures, off-rolling removes disadvantaged, disruptive or struggling pupils before they take their final exams, ensuring their results are not included in the school's statistics. Ofsted-commissioned research suggests 'that schools rated 'Inadequate' and 'Special Measures' are more likely to use off-rolling as well as being Academies or Local Authority Schools' (YouGov, 2019, p. 4). The key point is that, by driving education leaders towards ever-increasing efficiency and effectiveness, the system encourages time-saving processes to achieve particular outcomes, leading to results-oriented education; hence, schools are most likely to off-roll according to Ofsted when they have concerns about behaviour and academic achievement (YouGov, 2019, p. 5). Performance driven League Tables leave leaders susceptible to the newest educational fads promising greater efficiency.

Lastly, League Tables have unwittingly devalued exam results in the United Kingdom. As schools successfully rise to the challenge of improving their exam grades, the public and media declare that exams must be too easy, devaluing thousands of young people's efforts and achievements every year. Public and political opinion thus equates to increased numbers of young people achieving exam success with a deterioration in educational standards, without the realization of how many 'defective' children have been removed from the educational conveyor belt to achieve these results. This creates a catch-22 situation undermining educational leaders' efforts: the more successfully they improve exam results, the lower the public's perception of educational standards. In this conveyor-belt educational model, the more higher-grade exam results leaders achieve, the less valuable they are perceived to be.

2.3 Towards a new approach: understanding a system's history

For school leaders to think big and differently, they must understand that history matters in systems: their history, the school and community's history, and the education system's history. Those members of the school's community who have experience of before and during big policy shifts can differentiate between what was (the past) and what is (the present). But for those who come after a significant change, the new situation is their 'normal': they may not understand its heritage and influences.

Therefore, as we will go on to explore, leaders must consider how systems evolve, diverge and change in their school community. Taylorist thinking is focused on reducing a system to its component parts per the conveyer-belt approach, which often obscures its true nature, causing leaders to mistake one type of system for another. Such reductionism of the complexity of education and leadership is a key feature of this book's argument for why school leaders need to think big and think differently (see Figure 2.1).

2.4 System archetypes

The Cambridge Dictionary defines a system as "a set of connected things or devices that operate together" or "a set of organs or structures in the body that have a particular purpose" (Cambridge Dictionary). This definition reflects a conventional focus on the whole. However, because systems range from the very simple to the incredibly complex, this section outlines three of the four primary system archetypes to provide a contextual overview. These include simple, complicated and chaotic systems. I cover the fourth

Figure 2.1 Shifting mindsets from production line to systems.

type – complex adaptive systems, which I will suggest are most relevant to education – in the next chapter.

2.4.1 Simple systems

Since a simple system comprises a limited number of parts and interactions, an observer can generally predict the system's outcomes from its starting conditions. In nature, for example, we know that if a caterpillar eats a leaf, it will grow larger. This is an example of the most basic kind of simple system (Figure 2.2).

Riding a bike is another example of a simple system, this time involving several components. The wheels, frame, seat, chain, gears and rider come together to generate a faster mode of travel than walking. As with the caterpillar example, there is a clear cause and effect: the faster the cyclist pedals, the faster the bike travels. If the cyclist applies the brakes, the bike will slow and eventually stop. Thus, the cyclist provides the system's energy, and the human-bicycle interaction generates 'travel'. However, the moment the cyclist dismounts, the

Figure 2.2 Simple system.

interaction ends and the bike no longer travels. Thus, riding a bike can happen only when both rider and bike are combined, that is, the 'interaction' makes the system. However, simple systems seem so obvious that we are not necessarily conscious of them as systems.

This highlights an important aspect of identifying simple systems: we often do it instinctively, recognising a pattern of interaction without conscious thought. Simple systems typically involve direct, intuitive response mechanisms that render them self-explanatory; for example, if a cyclist applies more pressure to the pedals, the bike's speed quickly increases. The rapid responses in simple systems are one aspect which helps make them intuitive; you can feel the change and adjust. Learning in simple systems means we tend to sense and observe the requirements for engaging with a simple system.

An example of a simple system in an educational setting is taking the morning and afternoon registration. The teacher calls a name, and the named child replies "yes" to confirm they are present, requiring minimal instruction. A child who is new to the class's registration experience could quickly pick it up by observing their neighbours' response when their name is called. Since registration could not happen without a teacher to call names or children to respond, the combination of staff and children creates this simple system interaction.

Simple systems are often present but unrecognised in social interactions, partly due to their obviousness and partly because they are unconscious and habitual. Nevertheless, simple systems often underpin a school's everyday rituals and behaviours and shape the educational experience. Therefore, it is critical that leaders can spot them. An example I saw in one school was the deputy head's habit of snatching children's hats off them while they walked down the corridor, enforcing the school's no-hats rule (and promising to return their hats at the end of the school day). However, after pulling what she assumed was a hat off one girl's head, she discovered it was a hijab. The deputy head had clearly been in autopilot and apologised profusely. On reflection, I realised that the deputy head had at no point explained to me why so many children were wearing hats in her school, or why she felt it was her sole duty to remove them, and I had not asked – partly because her behaviour seemed so instinctive. Therefore, the ability to step back from the unconscious repetitive patterns inherent in simple systems is essential if leaders are to recognise and change their underlying causes.

Simple systems can thus have a collective effect. I remember being in one school whose staff lined up at the end of every afternoon to clap the children as they left. This simple system of gratitude showed clear cause-and-effect, with the students laughing and smiling in response to the staff clapping them. It also had a profound effect. It was evident watching the children that, no matter how the day had gone, they knew they would still be celebrated and smiling at the end of it. Moreover, parents waiting at the gate could witness how much the staff cared about their children and deemed them worthy of celebrating.

The direct cause-and-effect interactions that characterise simple systems like these also increase their manageability. For example, using lower-resistance wheels instantly makes a bike more efficient. However, the only way to increase the efficiency of a simple educational system such as taking the register is by calling the names out faster, which still depends on the child's response. Similarly, while a school could increase the efficiency of clapping its students by reducing the number who clap, freeing staff up for other duties, at what point does the interaction become less meaningful to staff and students? Decision-making in simple systems thus requires an understanding of how the system will react to change. What the cyclist or the teacher decides to do directly influences possible interactions in such simple systems.

To summarise, simple systems are characterised by a limited number of interacting parts, direct cause-and-effect and clearly identifiable energy inputs, for example, pushing pedals, clapping or pulling students' hats off. Furthermore, the system clearly terminates when the interaction ends, for example, the rider dismounts the bike, the deputy head stops removing hats or the clapping stops.

When dealing with simple systems, leaders must often decide how to make the system 'visible' and ensure good-quality interactions across its interacting parts. For example, a child with a hearing disability will not benefit from a teacher's effort to increase registration efficiency by calling out names faster. On the contrary, this would slow or invalidate the process. By prioritising completion speed over accuracy, the process no longer ensures all children are present and correctly accounted for and thus defeats the purpose. Leaders must ensure simple systems' instinctive nature does not lull staff into complacency, recognising that a focus on improving a system's parts at the cost of its interactions misses the nuances that shape systems. Moreover, school leaders must be vigilant against over-familiarisation with simple systems' patterns of interaction that undermine their system goals.

2.4.2 Complicated systems

In complicated systems, multiple components must work together to produce the same outcome. Figure 2.3 illustrates a larval reproduction cycle as an example of a complicated system: a larva emerges from an egg, becomes a caterpillar, undergoes metamorphosis, becomes a butterfly and lays an egg. This is defined as a complicated system because disruption to any one stage has consequences for the next one.

Another example of a complicated system is an aeroplane, comprising multiple components that must work sequentially or in parallel to produce the same outcome. Clearly defined relationships between its sequence components deliver clear cause and effect, for example, the engine builds momentum, providing enough thrust for the plane to take off. As the component interactions become familiar, the system demonstrates interaction reliability.

Getting to know systems 19

Complicated system

Figure 2.3 A complicated system.

Like simple systems, complicated systems are also reproducible and scalable. The interactions' repeatability becomes standardised, increasing the probability of the same result time and again, that is, the plane taking off and landing safely in this example, which is reassuring!

The reliability of a complicated system's interactions and outcomes is critical, necessitating a diagnostic approach when things go wrong to identify the point of failure. This involves backtracking through multiple components and interactions to find where the expected chain of interactions deviated and identifying the necessary adjustment. Once the interaction chain has been remedied, the complicated system's reliability is restored. Any changes to the sequence aim to increase the chain's efficiency or effectiveness, maximising the likelihood of the system reproducing the same outcome.

In an educational setting, the school-improvement approach arguably views schools as complicated machines in which 'fixing' a component (e.g., improving teachers' delivery of the curriculum) will improve exam results. National-level approaches often assume that schools need the right combination of components to guarantee an educational outcome in the system. By this logic, school leaders could abolish breaks to maximise learning time and increase the school's efficiency as a complicated system.

Although complicated systems retain the discernible cause-and-effect pathway of a simple system, they involve more interaction steps along the causal path. An example of a complicated system in an educational setting might be the logistical organisation of a school trip, requiring multiple interacting components to achieve a particular outcome. A school visit to the local museum might necessitate a series of steps, including sending information letters to parents, requiring signed consent forms to be returned, conducting a risk assessment of the journey and venue, informing pupils about what they need to bring on the day, allocating support staff for the trip and arranging transport to and from the museum. Each step in this sequence of events represents a component of the overall system. Consequently, if the school trip does not happen, it is possible to identify where the breakdown in the expected interaction chain occurred. For example, was the letter sent? Did parents return their consent forms? Did the risk assessment confirm the museum was safe for students and staff to visit? The more complicated the system, the more aware of its component interactions leaders must be to create the desired outcome.

School leadership also involves countless complicated systems, including curriculum standardisation, teaching assessments and behavioural rewards and sanctions. All depend on multiple components co-operating in a particular sequence to produce a desired outcome, for example, standardised lesson plans, improved learning outcomes or effective classroom management. School leaders manage this complicatedness through experience, recognizing the interactions and components through exposure to these systems.

A complicated system in a school aims to increase standardisation by reducing variance, thus ensuring outcome regularity. The In-Service Education Training (INSET) is a classic example, assuming that all those present will receive, understand and act on the information provided similarly. However, from my experience of delivering teacher training, outcomes can vary widely across a single staff cohort. While they may agree with the training material, variations in their experiences, service length and school roles mean there is no guarantee that exposure to the same training translates into standardised responses. Nevertheless, this ritual plays out across the country at the start of every school year.

An advantage of complicated systems is that they are well suited to hierarchical management structures, as different leaders can 'own' different aspects of the system at various organisational levels. Therefore, the school can appoint a manager to oversee a particular component, for example, school policy or curriculum delivery. This is where quality assurance and risk management are essential for leaders. From a conveyer-belt perspective, quality-assuring a product is necessary to meet customer or client expectations, that is, exam results. From an experience perspective, this involves learners and teachers maximising their understanding of the subject matter.

In theory, both simple and complicated systems can be deconstructed and reconstructed to produce a desired outcome, meaning that system components can be managed by different organisational levels with accountability for their function. Leaders who run a function in the system, whether a classroom, team, or department, are charged with maintaining its performance. As leaders progress up the hierarchy, their responsibilities may broaden (i.e., cover a greater section of the system's sequence) or deepen (i.e., more responsibility for the efficiency and effectiveness of a single system aspect). Such hierarchical organisation often creates top-down management styles that ensure staff perform the function's remit, for example, the maths department, administration team, physical education department. The higher leaders are in the hierarchy, the more they are expected to understand what is happening in their part of the (complicated) system.

One feature of component management in education is the introduction of new projects in schools – for example, introducing learning styles, using iPads, staff mediation – to test the viability of a particular outcome. Do learning styles improve engagement with curriculum materials? Do iPads enhance the learning experience, and do staff meditation sessions improve well-being? Projects are by their nature timebound, so part of the problem is not just the content but also how long is needed to assess a particular project's benefit to the system. School leaders can see such projects as a cog to add to the school machine's broader components. This raises the question of suitability, which we return to in Chapter 8. While it is important to determine whether a project is suited to a school's needs, it must also fit within the sequence of the relevant complicated system. Our key point is not the project itself but how it interacts with other parts of the system and in what sequence; these are crucial to ascertain.

Those implementing change in complicated systems generally assumes that altering individual system components will improve the system's overall performance. This is particularly evident in the current 'Red, Amber, Green' (RAG) rating system (or traffic light performance monitoring system – coincidentally this also comes from production lines), which deconstructs key aspects of a school's management system. The ubiquitous RAG matrix independently rates compartmentalised areas of a school, facilitating management discourse about the efficiency and effectiveness of each component. However, the interactions between components are rarely discussed. Rather, the improvement of an individual component is assumed to generate overall improvement in the system. School-improvement discourses focus on resource-and-requirement management to promote standardisation across the system. They implicitly assume that by championing 'consistency', the school will be more efficient and effective. School leaders often described this type of management as 'singing from the same hymn sheet', whereas now I would say 'working from the same conveyor-belt instruction manual', bringing us back to Taylor's legacy. Consistency is the antithesis of variance, which Taylor's management is responsible for reducing. With too many skilled artisans working on the conveyor belt, management loses control. However, there are alternative systems, such as chaotic.

2.4.3 Chaotic systems

When introduced to the term 'chaotic system', most people think of something messy, crazy, dysfunctional, impenetrable and hard to comprehend, that is, random disorder. Hence, many people assume that schools which are not efficient must be chaotic. To the untrained eye, a playgroup looks like absolute chaos! However, Chaos Theory, based on the work or Edward Lorenz (1917–2008), has a different take on it, showing that the apparent chaos in systems

22 Getting to know systems

previously assumed to be random states of disorder actually shows underlying patterns, feedback and interconnectedness.

2.4.3.1 Chaos Theory and the Butterfly Effect

Chaos Theory originated in Edward Lorenz's work on predicting weather conditions when he serendipitously discovered that data rounded to three decimal places produced radically different weather simulations than data rounded to six decimal places. This discovery demonstrated that small changes in initial conditions led to large differences in long-term outcomes, later described in the 1972 conference paper "Predictability: Does the Flap of Butterfly's Wings in Brazil Set off a Tornado in Texas?" Thereafter, this feature of chaotic systems was referred to as the 'Butterfly Effect', illustrated in Figure 2.4.

The Butterfly Effect describes a fundamental underlying principle of chaotic systems: a small change in the early stages of a chaotic system can result in a large change at a later stage. In short, the starting conditions matter. Unlike simple or complicated systems, chaotic systems are highly sensitive to initial conditions. This means they can be modified early in the system's life cycle, when they are most susceptible in their interplay with its wider environment.

An example of the early conditions affecting a school as a chaotic system happened years ago. I was part of the initial community consultation for one of the first Academies in England – defined as a school managed by a Trust (often sponsored through business) rather than the local government, with the argument being a new model would have potential for greater creative freedom for schools and improve parents' choice. The plan was to build a modern, award-winning architect-designed school on a new site in a predominantly affluent area. With one of the poorest council estates in London

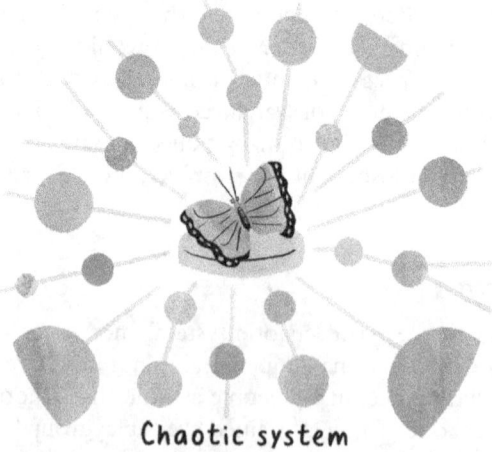

Figure 2.4 The beat of Butterfly's Wings in a chaotic system.

located only a few roads away, however, racial and class issues created a unique consultation dynamic. For some, the Academy would be a private school in all but name, whereas for others, it represented a good, easily accessible school for their children. The consultation thus concluded that the local community welcomed the new Academy but had substantially different expectations. The Academy was successfully established with a widely respected head teacher, recruiting new pupils each September until fully subscribed. Through the lens of a chaotic-system, the Academy was highly susceptible to early conditions, that is, public engagement with the local communities. These expectations of two different communities shaped the challenges the Academy would later face as the Academy became a feature of the local community.

2.4.3.2 Self-similarity: recognising patterns in apparent chaos

A second key feature of chaotic systems is their fractal structure. If we plotted a chaotic system's development, it would look far more haphazard than the straightforward cause-and-effect map characterising a simple or complicated system. However, it wouldn't be a completely random muddle either. Though interaction appears in what seems to unpredictable ways, the system's evolution would show a distinct form, referred to as a 'fractal': a shape that is self-similar at all scales. In Chaos Theory, this is called the law of self-similarity.

Snowflakes are a classic example of fractals and the law of self-similarity. Although every snowflake evolves a unique and unpredictable shape as it travels through the air's micro-conditions, its structure is a self-repeating pattern at all levels – an infinite nested structure at all scales. Fractal dimension is a measure of how a self-similar pattern is determined by its recurring interactions (dictated by the snowflake's microclimatic conditions) rather than its size.

We can use the example 'fractal' of a school hierarchy to illustrate the idea of fractal self-similarity in an educational setting, where the hierarchy takes a self-similar management shape: a head teacher supported by a leadership team of middle managers, each of which has a department of staff who manage smaller system components, for example, students, parents and supplies. Like a snowflake, the hierarchical structure repeats at every level.

From a cultural perspective, the leadership style can also exhibit self-similarity, replicating across a school community. For example, suppose a school's head teacher is a bully, and each leader in the hierarchy replicates the behaviour of the level above. In that case, a bullying culture will likely permeate at every level of the school community. Hence, focusing on bullying behaviour in classrooms or playgrounds misses the self-similarity replicated through the school's interactions at different levels of the school hierarchy. Since a chaotic system exhibits self-similarity throughout, system leaders must recognise that fractal behaviour is not confined to a team, class or individual but is evident in all aspects of the school when viewed as a chaotic system.

2.4.3.3 Unpredictable regularity

Another key feature of chaotic systems is that they show regularities without predictability. In a chaotic system, cause does not necessarily equal effect, nor can you confidently look at an effect and identify a cause. For example, we know that the weather will produce certain features, for example, rain or sunshine. However, we cannot predict with 100% accuracy when they will occur; we can only calculate their probability. This leads to a different type of system thinking: forecasting.

Forecasting involves predicting the *probability* of a system's possible outcomes. In the context of a school, leaders must be sensitive and responsive to changes as they implement new approaches, as they will be dealing with a range of possible outcomes rather than one guaranteed result. Unlike a complicated system where leaders already know the outcome, chaotic systems have recurrences which may be familiar but not certain. By being aware and practising system sensitivity, that is, what are changes in the pattern of the school, leaders can be alert to changes in the regularities of schools as a chaotic system.

For example, returning to the hypothetical school whose head teacher is a bully, we know that the conditions for bullying are present, but we do not know when an incident will occur or what it will involve. However, the established bullying hierarchy increases the probability of a bullying incident with high levels of predictability: if the head bullies the senior leadership team, the senior leadership team is likely to bully middle managers, middle managers are likely to bully teachers, teachers are likely to bully students and students are likely to bully each other. Although individual experiences may vary, the regularity of occurrence (of a bullying incident) is now a feature of the system.

2.4.3.4 System lock-in

The final feature of a chaotic system we will explore is system 'lock-in'. Once a chaotic system has matured, it is no longer sensitive to its initial conditions. Consequently, the system reproduces its behaviours with reliable regularity, regardless of environmental changes. Thus, it is 'locked in' to a pattern of interaction. In our theoretical example, the school's bullying culture will thus lock in over time.

Once system behaviour locks in occurs, it becomes a normalised system feature that is very difficult to undo. For example, when working with a school with high levels of bullying and conflict, Year 7 students (aged 11–12) expressed great concern to me about their school's bullying behaviour. In contrast, staff and older students (Years 8–11) had no concerns about this issue. I realised that the younger Year 7 students were the least desensitised to the bullying culture, whereas staff and older students had been exposed to it long enough that it became normalised. For me, it became apparent that the bullying culture had become normalised because it occurred at all levels, including students, staff and parents. Moreover, the head teacher felt bullied by the local community. In my mind, the school community's poor-quality interactions represented a chaotic system locked into a normalised behavioural pattern that was difficult to change. A change of leadership alone would not be enough, as patterns of interactions had become 'locked-in'.

Although there are undoubtedly many negative fractal patterns in education, there are also beneficial applications of chaotic systems thinking. As mentioned earlier, the staff in one school I visited gave the students a round of applause at the end of every day. As well as benefiting the students, this 'fractal' also increased staff well-being by weaving a nurturing thread through the school community. The head teacher and leadership team saw 'nurture' as a fundamental part of education: children were nurtured by staff, who were in turn nurtured by a leadership team engaged with parents and partners to nurture the school community, demonstrating self-similarity in a chaotic system.

2.5 Summary

This chapter introduced three system archetypes – simple, complicated and chaotic – and outlined the key features of each to help leaders understand the system with which they are engaging. By understanding a system's features and behaviour, school leaders will be better placed to think big and think differently about the change they want to implement, when there is the cry to "Change the System". Although much more could be said about all three, I now move to the fourth type – the Complex Adaptive System – and its importance to school communities and leaders seeking change. In doing so, I hope to move schools away from the legacy of Taylor and the dehumanising consequences this system has had on school leadership theory and toward a participatory co-construction of learning systems that can meet everyone's needs.

Notes

1 'I was put in a school isolation booth more than 240 times'. https://www.bbc.co.uk/news/education-47898657
2 https://educationinspection.blog.gov.uk/2019/05/10/what-is-off-rolling-and-how-does-ofsted-look-at-it-on-inspection/

3 Complex adaptive systems

The previous chapter covered three types of systems: simple, complicated and chaotic. I now introduce a fourth type: the Complex Adaptive System (CAS). This chapter will start with exploring Complex Systems in the natural world before applying them to social systems and schools in particular.

Let us begin by looking first at complex systems in the natural sciences; this will help us later to see how they differ in the social sciences and consider the implications for educational leaders. We will then explore the key features of a complex adaptive system: feedback, self-organisation, boundaries and time.

3.1 Complexity in the natural sciences

When seeking to find complex adaptive systems (CASs) in nature it is important to look for two features: interconnection and interdependency. Interconnection, as in other systems, is self-evident: to be part of a system, you must be connected to it. The second aspect means that unlike our simple or complicated systems, dependency is not sequential but rather co-existing and exchanging continuously, hence inter-dependent. Examples of CASs in the natural sciences can include for example beehives and ant colonies, where there are interactions and interdependency between the complex system and its parts. What is important is the interactions between things rather than the individual parts and how they function. As such, the hive or ant colony can be identified as a superorganism whose features depend on the totality of interactions rather than the system's components. For example, an ant colony's tunnels function as the collective 'lungs' to clear waste gases for the entire ant population; because the ants maintain the tunnels and the tunnels maintain the ants, the interaction is interdependent.

Another example of interdependency within a CAS is human consciousness, that is, our awareness of who we are and our place in the universe. Because consciousness does not reside in any single part of the brain (or even body), consciousness is not a component feature. Instead, the totality of interactions within our bodies produces an overall system state which is not determined by any single bodily component. Consciousness is thus a feature of huge array of interdependent interactions creating a feature in us as a complex system. Importantly, since consciousness is a feature of the human condition greater than the sum of its parts, it cannot be 'located' by deconstructing the human brain. Indeed, trying to break down complex systems into individual components may undermine the very thing we seek to explore.

The scale of CAS can be from the brain to the size of cities. Just touching on the social sciences for an instant, in urban planning and geography, a city's relationship to its environment is another example of a CAS. Hence, the inhabitants' consumption of environmental resources (e.g., air, water and soil) shapes and modifies the city, changing the environment in turn. We rarely think about how cities influence our day-to-day lives and vice versa. Air pollution is an excellent example of a feature determined by a city's interdependencies. While our individual choices in buying a particular car brand contribute to the system's air pollution, the combined interactions of these choices create a complex system independent of any single person, family or community. Other features will contribute to the interactions such as the density of the buildings, the climate, the planting of trees and green spaces, factories and industrial pollution. All of these interactions create or mitigate against air pollution through the interdependencies in the system.

3.1.1 Understanding complexity in the natural sciences

Natural scientists use various methodologies to understand the complex systems present in nature. While mathematical models or computer simulations enable the inclusion of a range of system features, they cannot encapsulate the entire system. Instead, an appropriate systems model distils the key dynamic interactions, representing the system's behaviour as fully as possible. By system behaviour we can say what are the reoccurring features and, alternatively, what is changing in once stable patterns in our system of interest. Complex models and simulations allow natural-sciences researchers to map and potentially predict how complex systems are likely to behave, testing the relative importance of system interactions in determining the features of interest of further exploration. This can be how a plant adapts to find sources of light as in Figure 3.1.

3.1.2 Complexity theory as a multi-discipline science

Natural scientists have used Complexity Theory to show how system changes – especially human interventions – can have unintended consequences and hidden benefits in the natural world. Importantly, Complexity Theory is an umbrella term for the range of concepts used to investigate complex phenomena, rather than a single theory. A pivotal moment for Complexity Theory came about in the 1970s, when the Santa Fe Institute brought together a group of interdisciplinary academics to understand complex phenomena by using computers to model complexity and simulate the rules governing a particular complex system. More recently Complexity Theory as a multi-disciplinary science continues to address the challenges our planet faces,

28   *Complex adaptive systems*

Complex system

Figure 3.1 A natural system of complexity.

Syukuro Manabe, Klaus Hasselmann and Giorgio Parisi went on to win the 2021 Novel Prize for Physics, summarised on the Nobel Prize's website:

> The Earth's climate is one of many examples of complex systems. Manabe and Hasselmann are awarded the Nobel Prize for their pioneering work on developing climate models. Parisi is rewarded for his theoretical solutions to a vast array of problems in the theory of complex systems.[1]

The use of Complexity Theory in a growing range of sciences provides a lens for seeing the world in a way to understand the interconnected and interdependent nature of systems. Let us now look at Complexity in the social sciences.

3.1.3 *Complexity theory in the social sciences*

While applying Complexity Theory in the natural and mathematical sciences has provided new insights into the physical world around us, the social sciences have been less ready to adopt its approach. This is partly a result of misperceptions of what 'complexity' means in this context, since most people assume it must be too complicated and inaccessible for non-mathematicians. On the contrary, I would argue that Complexity Theory is implicit in many social science disciplines, including psychology, anthropology, criminology and education. Indeed, leading complexity theorists Byrne and Callaghan (2014) distinguished between *restricted* complexity, where researchers computationally model a limited subset of variables to test their interrelationships, and *general* complexity, which explores how such models can help us understand reality. As systems leaders, we are interested in the latter. We don't need a mathematical model of a classroom to understand its complexity; we just need to be able to look at it through the lens of a complex systems framework. Thus, part of the opportunity of using Complexity Theory is distinguishing between its natural and social-sciences applications. As such, we will define Complexity Theory and its approach in a social-sciences context for our purposes:

> A framework to understand social systems phenomena such as schools, which have the interactive and interdependent features of feedback, self-organisation, emergence, system boundaries, and the relativity of time.[2]

These five features enable us to develop a framework for engaging with complex systems in social settings such as schools. System recognition is particularly relevant to understanding how humans organise things and the way this evolves. However, education and educational research are yet to fully engage with complex approaches, but some have started to apply (Davies [2004]; Davis, B., and Sumara, D., [2006]; Osberg, D., Biesta, G., & Cilliers P. [2008]; Mason, M. [2008]), which require recognising and understanding how schools can be viewed as complex adaptive systems. The component mindset creates the perception of a boundary between teaching and learning as separate, distinct and discrete, yet from a system lens, they are very much interconnected and interdependent. Therefore, when look at educational philosophy, educational research and educational practice they are all potential congruent with complexity theory because learning is about *dynamics* – the interplay of relationships from neurons to classrooms (see Figure 3.2).

The history of schools is over 2,000 years old. The first recorded 'school' (The Shishi High School) emerged in China in 141 BC, as a place specifically for education; in the United Kingdom it wasn't until some 700 years later that

Figure 3.2 Seeing complexity in schools.

England established its first school (the King's School, Canterbury, established in 597 AD). In addition to the institutions, educational ideas are rooted in history, which influences how we perceive and recognise teaching and learning in our current system. History matters because humans are a story-telling species that uses narratives to make sense of the world and see patterns in randomness. Thus, our stories preserve culture by passing collective perceptions, beliefs and interpretations from one generation to another. Why? Because each culture, local and national, perpetuates its own unique, historical narrative, meaning that social diffusion was infinitely slower across geographical and cultural boundaries than within them. History in social systems tells us where we have come from and what we are doing now. Importantly, for system leaders, recognising the history of the school and its community enables them to appreciate what is already of importance and where there is likely to be challenge and resistance. In one school I was in, years ago, there was a strong seafaring culture with pictures of sailors and boats across the corridors. The environment reflected this history, and clearly, over time, this had created a hyper-masculine culture in the staff; this made it difficult for female staff to be heard in meetings or progress into leadership positions.

Now more than ever, leaders must adopt a systems perspective to address the challenges facing schools and their communities. Educational research (and the social sciences generally) has arguably fallen into the mechanical way of thinking about schools and organisational change laid down by history. Consequently, educational leaders often manage systems 'blind', relying on intuition rather than benefiting from a guidebook of conceptual frameworks that would help them recognise and navigate different system types and engage effectively with complexity.

To begin providing this guidance, this chapter introduces the key ingredients of a complexity approach – which were defined earlier as feedback, self-organisation, boundaries and time – to help leaders understand how to think big and think differently about school change.

3.2 Key features of complex adaptive systems

3.2.1 Feedback

We generally understand feedback in everyday life as a response to or opinion about someone else's work or idea, usually to help improve it. In *systems* feedback, however, a process's outputs (consequences) regulate its subsequent rate/productivity. Two types of feedback are involved, referred to in Complexity Theory as 'positive' (feedback that amplifies systems outputs, resulting in growth or decline) and 'negative' (feedback that dampens outputs, stabilising the system at a point of equilibrium). For clarity, I will use the terms *amplification* (positive feedback) and *regulation* (negative feedback), exploring both in greater detail below.

3.2.1.1 Amplification

According to the Cambridge English Dictionary, *amplify* means 'to increase the size or effect of something'. In social systems, amplification thus represents how the system increases social energy through its network structures (see Figure 3.3).

Amplification arguably originates from two sources: external and internal. In external amplification, an external catalyst affects the system, which then amplifies the catalyst's energy internally. For example, a school whose recent inspection raised concerns around online safety might reasonably respond with assemblies, class plans, cross-curricular activities and parental information letters to raise online-safety awareness across the school community. In this example, the inspection was the external catalyst, but the school subsequently amplified the catalyst's 'energy' across different stakeholder groups – and thus across the whole system.

In the second form of amplification, internal relationships begin clustering and connecting at different systemic levels, generating internal amplification. A hypothetical example is a school council member who becomes increasingly concerned about cyberbullying in their year group and raises it with the school council. In turn, the school council informs the head teacher, who takes it to her senior leadership team. As a result, the school develops various prevention materials, adjusts its policies to support students in reporting cyberbullying, establishes parents' workshop and recruits external experts to help staff understand the latest cyberbullying trends and issues. Thus, the amplification is self-generated within the school. The network of social relationships

Figure 3.3 Amplification.

32 Complex adaptive systems

facilitating transmission throughout the system is a key feature of this self-generation. We will look at networks in more detail later in this chapter.

Amplification can also work in the opposite direction, amplifying the effects of an unfavourable catalyst toward a less advantageous school culture. I remember a distinct social divide in one staffroom I visited, for example. It transpired that an older male staff member had spoken to a younger female colleague in a rather abrupt and harsh way. The resulting tension affected not only their relationship but also the team and department, ultimately leading to a polarisation of the school's staff. Thus, the school's social networks amplified the catalyst incident's effect, creating a decisive split between staff who felt the male teacher was right and those who supported the female staff member. For systems leaders, it is critical to understand that amplification is a crucial feature of a complex adaptive system. Recognising the types of amplification happening in the school is essential for identifying and engaging with it.

3.2.1.2 Regulatory feedback

Regulatory feedback is the second major type of system feedback, ensuring that a system performs or survives within a range acceptable for its functional needs. As mentioned earlier, Complexity Theory often refers to regulatory feedback as 'negative'. However, this does not mean that it is always undesirable, only that it regulates the system by dampening of aspects of the system which may amplify – just like a dam slows a river's flow (see Figure 3.4).

Examples of regulatory feedback include, arguably, adhering to government legislation to meet teachers' pay and conditions, ensuring school buildings are safe for the school community and/or ensuring the correct grading criteria are used for exam papers. All of these examples indicate that the various school systems are regulating a range of functional needs. whereas if they were allowed to be amplified, teachers' pay would drain the budget, lack of building inspections would make schools dangerous and grades would be based on the subjective perspective of the teacher. When identifying regulatory feedback in your setting, it is essential to understand how a system

Figure 3.4 Regulatory feedback.

currently uses regulatory capacities to prevent amplification overwhelming the system and allowing regulation to develop with in adequate range. We could call this 'system tolerances', that is, what is permissible in the system before it requires regulating. Punitive behaviour management policies use regulatory feedback to keep behaviour within acceptable limits by escalating punishments in response to breaches (amplification of unwanted behaviours) of these limits. Thus, regulatory feedback aims to return the system to its functional state (where teachers can teach and students can learn) by standardising behaviour and return to an acceptable system tolerance.

A second aspect of regulatory feedback occurs when the system responds to internal amplification to limit the level of change within the school. For example, teachers might address the amplification of bullying in a year group by monitoring specific pupils, responding early to student/parental concerns and dealing swiftly with bullying incidents. In this way, the system regulates potential amplification within the year group to return it to a functional state. Regulatory feedback can often be mistaken for linear cause-and-effect, that is, if leaders do X, they will achieve Y. However, systems leaders recognise that when you instigate a change, seeking to tip the system into a new way of being, regulatory feedback is a natural response. Such feedback ensures schools do not become susceptible to every educational fashion or fad, such that the system regulates itself. Hence, through regulatory feedback, the system protects itself from environmental pressures and any associated external catalysts that pressure the system to change. Identifying these regulatory features is one of the key challenges of systems leadership.

3.2.2 Self-organisation: from individuals to networks

What creates a network in a school or community? A network is typically preceded by a need or interest delineating those who share it as a distinct and identifiable group. For example, school staff may want to address the retention of newly qualified teachers. While team leaders or department heads may have a similar interest in this respect, they might not have reached out to each other yet. In this way, they are a collection of individuals who have yet to identify a common interest. The next stage would be to signal that they have this interest either in a meeting or as part of less formal staff interactions. For example, a colleague Mrs Green might raise an issue that Mr Purple had also been concerned about in his department, which is the ability to retain newly qualified teachers. The concern raised by Mrs Green prompts Mr Purple to send a message flagging their shared interest, as this is also a concern for him. At this point, the actors recognise their shared interest – I refer to the initial individuals as 'bounded actors', as they have started to become bound about a particular issue, concern or challenge.

Once we start to see connections – in the case of Mrs Green and Mr Purple through communication – we can turn to Hebb's Rule (1949). Hebb was one the pioneers of neuroscience and how the biology of the brain worked, particularly networks of neurons. Hebb's Rule explains how networks are formed via the weight of interaction: the more interaction, the stronger the "weight" of connection is, or as Hebb famously said, "Cells that fire together, wire together". In the example shown in Figure 3.5, Mr Purple sends a message to Mrs Green asking if she, too, is concerned about the retention of newly qualified staff, the equivalent of both 'firing together'. Mrs Green has not acknowledged Mr Purple's message at this point, so the weight of connection is low because a message sent is not yet a message acknowledged; there is a one-directional connection.

Mrs Green replies that she is also concerned about the retention of newly qualified staff at the school, to which Mr Purple responds with a sigh of relief! See Figure 3.6. The weight of interaction has now become two-directional: the sent message is received, eliciting a response. It is crucial for systems leaders to understand that it is not enough just to send out messages and assume the recipients understand the intent. Importantly, the weight of interaction is now increasing as 'connecting' occurs.

In Figure 3.7, Mr Purple signals that he has received Mrs Green's message and continues the conversation on retaining newly qualified teachers. Now we see what Hebb described as the 'weight of interaction' increasing from Mrs Green, which is establishing a two-directional connection at this stage.

In Figure 3.8, Mrs Green responded to Mr Purple, establishing a relationship via the weight of interaction between them. Their interactions have formed a topic-based network of two in which they signal and respond to each other. The next stage is to reach out to other bounded actors with the same common interest.

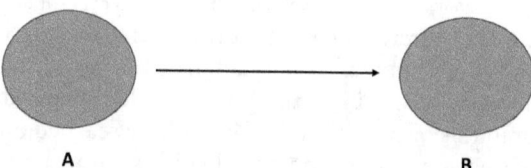

Figure 3.5 Teacher A (Mr Purple) sends a message to teacher B (Mrs Green).

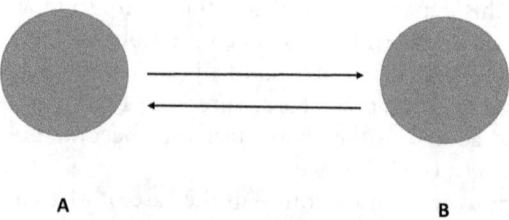

Figure 3.6 Teacher B (Mrs Green) responds to Teacher A (Mr Purple).

Figure 3.7 Teacher A (Mr Purple) continues the conversation with Teacher B (Mrs Green).

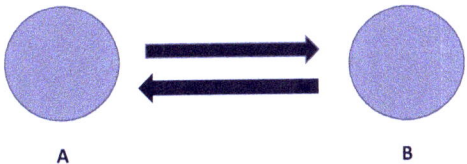

Figure 3.8 The weight of interaction between teachers has been established.

Based on Hebb's Rule, we have thus established that interaction on a topic 'retaining newly qualified teachers', which has bounded the actors in this particular network. Importantly, the topic is not important to system leaders but rather to understanding how interactions create self-organising networks. As we have seen, individuals become bound through a common aspect; this communicating creates connections with weights of interaction which can increase over time, as others join, and a network is formed. System leaders can now understand how self-organisation is shaping the interplay of complex systems such as schools. This leads to our next focus: the network's *shape*.

3.2.3 Network shapes

A network may comprise many individuals, whether a class, peer group or teaching department. As systems leaders, however, we are more interested in the *shape* of the network than the individual personalities that it comprises. Network shapes tell system leaders about how bounded actors have organised themselves. To illustrate this, I will explore three primary network shapes, which I first came across in the work of Davis and Sumara (2006): the hub-and-spoke network, the loose network and the meshed network See Figure 3.9 below. Each has its own particular advantages and disadvantages, which we will explore. Let's begin with what I think is the most common network shape in educational settings, the hub-and-spoke.

3.2.3.1 The hub-and-spoke network

A hub-and-spoke network resembles a bicycle wheel, with a central element (e.g., a person, team or function within a school) connected to multiple

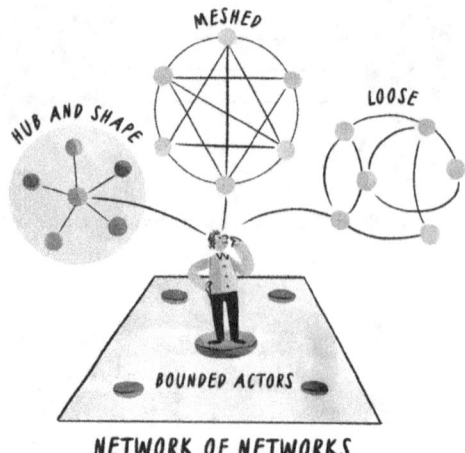

Figure 3.9 Network shapes.

surrounding spokes. The central hub generates the system's energy (see Chapter 4, on forms of system energy), coordinating and distributing information to the surrounding spokes, which use it to implement changes where possible. Crucially, however, the spokes do not communicate with each other in this type of network. Although communication can be one-directional (with the hub transmitting to the spokes) or two-directional (when the spokes respond to the hub), information flows only *from or to the hub*. As the gatekeeper of resources and communication, the hub thus acts as the amplifier or regulator of network changes.

In schools, hubs standardise behaviour by applying uniform performance criteria across the spokes. However, this can be problematic for the spokes if there is no acknowledgement of the environment in which they must perform. Such cases often lead to variance, with each spoke adapting to its particular environmental conditions. Moreover, the spokes' access to hub-controlled resources often depends on their performance. For hubs, there are challenges in ensuring equitable resource allocation between spokes, particularly as some resources may benefit certain spokes but disadvantage others due to differences in environmental conditions. Existing hubs may also connect to new spokes, in which case the network shape is sustainable as long as the hub can maintain resources and coordination. However, when a hub begins failing, spokes may simply leave the network rather than seek connection with each other due to this centralised network shape.

3.2.3.2 Loose networks

In a loose network, all network actors are linked. However, the connections are primarily *indirect*; most actors have only a few direct connections, while a small number are highly linked. Communication can thus cluster around members with a high weight of interaction, particularly as there is no central hub controlling the information pathway, and actors can reach out to each other to independently generate new connections and increase the weight of interactions. A feature of this type of network shape is that information is distributed organically, that is, through self-organisation. Since members may operate in multiple environments – for example, staff across various departments coming together to address cross-curricular activities for student year groups – network members may have greater access to opportunities across the school to develop activities together.

Years ago, I was fortunate to co-found a London-wide network of local authorities who wanted to develop anti-bullying initiatives using restorative practice. It began with only two of us but soon expanded to over 13 members across different local authorities. Interestingly, there was no chair, and those attending decided the agenda on the day. While attendance varied, a smaller core group emerged who regularly attended. Although this network shape may have benefited the network members, it did not produce any tangible system change in itself. Maybe that was not its point, however. Instead, the network provided a sense of belonging and identity to roles that could feel relatively isolated within their respective systems. The connective energy allowed members to share ideas and perspectives, returning to their schools and communities feeling more invigorated. In the absence of the central coordinator that typifies a hub-and-spoke model, the network met the loose network's emerging needs rather than prescribing requirements.

3.2.3.3 Meshed networks

Unlike a loose network, where most actors have only a few direct links but have opportunities to connect with others, a meshed network (also known as a 'dense' network) has more equally distributed connections. A meshed network is distinguished by its high connectivity between all network actors, meaning that everyone tends to know everything simultaneously. Consider a social media group like a parent WhatsApp group, for example. The members can all send and receive messages, knowledge is known to all simultaneously; hence, the network has a high level of interaction meshing it together. Like loose networks, meshed networks do not have a central control hub. Instead, information passes rapidly through the network due to the high exchange levels between actors and the high weight of interactions. As a consequence, this can create shoaling effects where actors rapidly replicate the behaviour of their neighbours, just as large groups of fish change direction at what appears to the same time or we hear the murmuration of swallows in the sky. Humans also display such shoaling behaviour. The UK's Great Toilet Paper Shortage in 2020 is a perfect example. This crisis was not caused by a resource deficit, since there was ample toilet paper for the nation's needs. Instead, national and social media reports about the COVID-19 pandemic amplified bulk-buying behaviour through communication networks, and watching others hoarding in supermarkets caused in-store shortages. Rather than being led by a single actor, the meshed network took effect.

The same effects of a meshed network might be seen in an In Service Education and Training (INSET) group discussing a new school initiative. The group may fix on a positive or negative response, affecting their group behaviour (as a meshed network) in either endorsing or challenging the proposed change. Importantly, meshed networks can also be unlimited in their scale, enabling people to connect and communicate so quickly and easily that they can potentially incorporate an infinite number of actors. Hence the teacher INSET group could rapidly grow, with neighbouring school staff attending, or colleagues from partner schools.

For systems leaders, therefore, meshed networks present an opportunity to instigate rapid group change. A meshed network's decentralised features enable mass communication to shape network decisions and outcomes rapidly. Moreover, the density of connections leads to shoaling effects, with connected actors quickly replicating one another's behaviour. However, this same strength can also prove a weakness; if the wrong information is transmitted in a meshed network, it becomes contagious. The high connectivity means it disseminates quickly through the group. Nevertheless, meshed networks are highly resilient to losing individual actors, with energy and knowledge stored in the whole rather than in the parts. Thus, losing any single actor does not affect overall behaviour in a meshed network.

3.2.3.4 Social eco-systems: a network of networks

The final network to discuss is the combination of all three types together with bounded actors, who belong to a 'network of networks'. This is when there is the presence of the same type of network shape present in the complex system, such as a multiple hub-and-spokes or, more often, diversity of network shapes in the school – for example, staff friendship groups, curriculum planning team and school council.

For example, a system leader in a school may simultaneously belong to a hub-and-spoke model involved in teaching standards, a meshed network concerned with staff well-being, a loose network comprising the student chess club, and have a bounded interest in systems change in schools. This diversity of network shapes enables an eco-system's resiliency to environmental forces.

While a complex adaptive system may initially take any network shape, it is not fixed and immutable; its form can always change. Therefore, complex adaptive systems can adjust to meet the survival needs identified by their leaders. For a complex adaptive system to change its network shape, systems leaders need to change the network's current interaction weights. For example, a hub-and-spoke network could evolve into a loose network if the system leader's hub encourages greater inter-spoke communication and less reliance on coordination. Similarly, a meshed network could morph into a hub-and-spoke network if a particular network actor or group becomes increasingly influential, such that other actors spend less time communicating with each other and more with that one person. It is the weight of interaction that influences the network shape's adaptability.

Finally, in understanding the importance of network shapes, it is critical to recognise that a network is greater than the sum of its parts. We are not interested in a network's individuals but in the shape of its connective whole. However compelling, powerful personalities or concerns about dysfunctional teams and the natural churn of a school's community are not under analysis here. Instead, systems leaders must understand the network's formation and shape, which determine how those in the network communicate and behave. By analysing different network shapes, systems leaders can identify the weight of interactions and how they are forged in social systems, helping them to think big and think differently about their school's networks.

3.2.4 Emergence

The combination of network shapes, and their ability to self-organise as well as give feedback (amplification and regulation), leads to another key feature of complex adaptive systems: emergence. Unlike a system component, emergence occurs through interaction and interconnection, which enable those in the system to see or do something new in the system (see Figure 3.10). For example, a school's culture is an emergent feature of all the interactions that happen on a daily basis.

Consider your school's culture for a moment. How do you know it exists? If I were to speak to one person in the school, would I 'know' the school's culture? If I read the school policy or observed a lesson, could I accurately

Figure 3.10 Emergence.

identify the school's culture? It is doubtful, since culture exists in the totality of interactions that happen every day and can change depending on those interactions. Emergence is the ability of a school to do something new or different. Therefore, emergence is fundamental to a social system's ability to adapt.

Systems leaders will experience emergence in two ways: organic and intentional. In organic emergence, a new feature emerges from interactions in a school, for example, students' interest in improving the local environment might lead to litter pickups around the school that parents and staff support. However, organic emergence can be challenging since it occurs both spontaneously and consequentially rather than intentionally, but still changes system behaviour. This is because emergence depends on all features of complex adaptive systems: feedback, network shapes, boundaries and time. Therefore, system leaders must be sensitive to changes in the school since these are where unintended consequences and new opportunities can arise. Rather than changing individual behaviour, system sensitivity is thus about recognising that changes in interactions and interdependencies (e.g., the loss of a classroom or the influx of a different cohort of students) also change the school's culture of emergent possibilities.

In the second type – intentional emergence – system leaders deliberately set the *conditions* for emergence but, critically, not the *outcome*. To establish the right conditions for emergence, systems leaders must change feedback, network shapes, boundaries and the experience of time. Intentional emergence thus necessitates approaches that go against traditional forms of school leadership, particularly embracing uncertainty (not knowing what might happen next) and, consequently, being comfortable with ambiguity (that something, anything or nothing could happen). Hence, a system leader's skill in creating intentional emergence is ultimately dependent on their willingness to study the patterns of interactions maintaining the system's current state and identify the unique conditions necessary for enabling new emergent behaviour. For me, the power of intentional emergence is in generating the conditions for a school community to create something new that matters to them.[3]

Although emergence requires system energy (discussed in the next chapter), it can amplify the imagining of new possibilities and ways of being in the school. By overcoming boundaries and enabling new connections, emergence can in turn pave the way for more emergent change.

As the ability to predict when emergence will occur is relative to other system features, emergence creates ambiguity and uncertainty. Arbitrary timelines for change often fail in schools for two reasons. Firstly, timelines do not account for feedback and network changes, often stifling the opportunity for emergence. Secondly, timelines restrict emergent features' to the earliest need to achieve an outcome rather than allowing the emergent feature to mature. Assuming that a system such as a school can achieve change instantly fails to recognise a complex adaptive system's needs.

Chapter 8 will return to the challenge for system leaders in sustaining emergence in schools.

3.2.5 Boundaries

Boundaries delineate what is inside and outside the system. However, this may be a deceptively simple statement, as determining what is in and outside a system can be very challenging. General Systems Theory identifies two types of system: closed and open. Closed systems have a high level of predictability because they do not exchange anything other than energy with their environment; they are self-contained. For example, putting a lid on a kettle turns it into a closed system, since it can only exchange energy (heat) with its surrounding environment, not water vapour (matter). It is hard to find these in real life. On the other hand, open systems are engaged in constant exchanges with their environment, for example, information, matter, people, items or energy. For example, skin is excellent at keeping our insides from falling out but still allows us to exchange water (sweat) and air (breath) with our environment. Therefore, understanding types of boundaries in open systems is important for identifying what passes into the system and what remains outside.

In schools, reception desks and guest passes are a common form of boundary-setting, ensuring that random members of the public cannot enter the school without permission. Instead, a visitor must sign in, with access based on the system's ability to identify people, filtering those who are acceptable in the system. Physical boundaries are the simplest type; a school's physical boundaries define its spatial parameters, which can be further demarcated into shared spaces (e.g., classrooms) and restricted spaces (e.g., the staff room) for particular stakeholders. Maintaining physical boundaries requires system energy, with failures obvious to see, cracks in the celling or unhinged doors.

Though not physical, perceived boundaries are constructs created in the human mind and can feel just as real (see Figure 3.11). Implicit system rules and professional mindsets can create such perceived boundaries. Examples include staffroom territorialism such as designated seating areas for particular groups based on perceived professional hierarchy, for example, PE teachers tending to sit separately from maths teachers, who might commandeer the couch. Perceived boundaries help in-group members know whether they are within acceptable limits and delineate outgroup members as external, kept outside the social network.

Perceived boundaries most often manifest as disapproval. Once created, the in-group reinforces the boundary by disapproving of those seeking to leave and rejecting those seeking to enter. Thus, perceived boundaries often remain hidden when school leaders set out the organisation's values, defining what is inside and outside their vision and principles. For this reason, we must interpret a value's *meaning* rather than rely on its label. I have worked in many schools advocating generic values such as respect, compassion and aspiration without actually defining them. When this happens, individual members of the school community must rely on their understanding of the *label*, which can vary enormously, meaning there is no uniform *definition* and thus *understanding* of the boundaries which contain the value. This leads to ambiguity and

Figure 3.11 Real and perceived boundaries.

confusion. Without a clearly defined meaning to demarcate the value's explicit boundaries, it becomes open to interpretation, rendering it valueless.

3.2.5.1 Boundaries in schools

Part of the challenge in achieving sustainable change in schools is identifying the implicit boundaries that need modifying or dismantling. Where a boundary seems impassable, there may be a workaround. In the same way that a well-trodden shortcut to avoid a gate becomes more visible, worn and thus normalised, a workaround can quickly become ritualised as school members pursue a particular goal. Suppose staff cannot use a colour photocopier in the staffroom, for example. In that case, they may resort to printing colour pictures in the art department, where a printer is connected to the school intranet. Such workarounds allow ingroup members to continue a particular system behaviour while maintaining a rule for everyone else.

Boundary creation and maintenance can arise from what the system continuously rejects or does not give feedback on. For example, a school claiming to be inclusive that continually excludes students with special educational needs or disabilities undermines its declared value. This apparent inconsistency may be because the school has an implicitly narrow definition of 'inclusion', or because its definition of 'inclusion' is so broad that its covers multiple additional categories, that is, the school may consider itself inclusive *despite* excluding a particular group. Boundary maintenance is a form of power in socially complex adaptive systems. Those imposing boundaries, those defending boundaries and those opting out all have a particular form of power. System leaders need to recognise how boundaries come about and are maintained in their system. For example, the *absence* of sexual-harassment education, confidential referral pathways or processes to recognise incidences represents system inaction, for students who may be being sexually harassed. Thus, the boundary is between doing something and doing nothing. As I said at the beginning, deciding what is inside and outside of the system is challenging.

The norms, rituals, beliefs and narratives that make up a school's culture also create boundaries. Hence, system leaders must be aware of their own perceived limits and play with shifting them to see the potential for new opportunities. Reflecting on how a school's culture influences our boundaries helps us recognise that we are not separate from it but an integral, immersive part of shaping and maintaining it. In doing so, we can understand why boundaries exist, where they do, and how shifting them can change feedback and network structures, unlocking opportunities for emergent features in the school.

3.2.6 Time

Since the concept of 'time' is such a hefty one, this section does not attempt to cover the depth of research and thinking around it. Instead, we will focus on what time means in complex adaptive systems. In simple and complicated systems, time moves in one direction because the system seeks to produce an outcome. Therefore, time is sequential, that is, students must gather in the playground before queueing up and moving through the corridors to get to class. This one-way direction is referred to as the 'arrow of time', meaning that one thing cannot happen before another: time is linear. However, other forms of time also occur in schools.

For example, the English school calendar is based on the *circle* rather than the *arrow* of time. The school calendar was originally based on the cyclical rhythms of the farming seasons because families needed their children to help with the summer harvest. This form of time is now so ingrained in the education system that a school that seeks to change it is considered radical. The circle of time is based on natural reoccurring rhythms in nature. For those with a lengthy career, the education system itself can feel like a cyclical rhythm, with politics continually rehashing and reinventing the same issues, such as giving school leaders more freedom to raise standards, then the concern that standards are falling and there needs to be more oversight. Thus, fads and educational fashions come and go in ways that start to feel cyclical with enough time spent in a system such as schools.

The final aspect of the complexity approach recognises that time is relative in socially complex adaptive systems such as schools (see Figure 3.12).

By relative, I mean that time is experienced through the interconnections between different aspects of the system. Thus, for change to occur in a school, multiple aspects of the system must connect and self-organise to create emergence. Moreover, the experience of time that it takes to do this depends on perceptions of time within the system, not on the arrow of time. For example, suppose students concerned about climate change raise it with their class representatives, who take it to the school council. Let's assume the school

44 Complex adaptive systems

Figure 3.12 The relativity of school time.

council suggests that staff should receive training about climate-ready classrooms, and the head teacher agrees. But because staff INSET must be booked in advance, it takes a year before there is space in the school calendar or staff to receive appropriate training on preparing climate-ready classrooms. For this scenario, perceptions of time between the students request and the result of enabling a staff INSET will depend on the perceiver's position in the system. The head teacher may feel that they are moving very quickly to enable staff to respond, whereas the students may feel that this is too slow in addressing a climate emergency. For example, the conversation between the class representatives and the school council may seem fast given rapid amplification through the network. However, finding an appropriate time to deliver the training may seem slow from a student's perspective – while from the head teacher's perspective, it is the earliest available slot for ensuring all staff can be fully trained. Consequently, the students perceive the school to be slow in meeting their requirements on this issue, whereas staff perceive the system as moving quickly to meet student needs.

System-based perceptions of time can become boundaries in themselves, for example, staff complaining that they do not have time to do certain things. Here, systems leaders must distinguish between the system's available energy for doing things and the time those things take, which is relative. School initiatives and pilots often claim to achieve school change within one to three years, yet research typically describes school changes happening within five to seven years (Miles, 1964; Georgiades and Phillimore, 1975). In a more recent literature review by Thompson on school change (2010) she concludes that a key area of agreement on school change is that it "takes time, longer than anticipated" (2010:71). When engaging with schools as complex adaptive systems, the key point is that change is *relative*; the answer depends on the system's ability and need to generate feedback, self-organise into appropriate network shapes, facilitate emergence, and shift or change boundaries. Thus, depending on urgency and stakeholder power, perceptions of how quickly or slowly the present system transitions to the desired state may differ (I will return to this point in Chapter 7).

For system leaders, understanding time as a relative concept explains why, when a school experiences a significant trauma, it can be particularly difficult to instigate change; trauma becomes a memory that anchors the school community to a particular moment in time, making it difficult to move on. Alternatively, past success can also become an 'anchor in time', keeping the school in the past moment of joy and satisfaction, rather than fully acknowledging the present or recognising what the future could hold, such that time is experienced compared to a particular moment of trauma or success. This is partly why history matters so much in social systems such as schools, since it indicates how and when the school experienced different time states. For systems leaders, thinking big and thinking differently require them to consider time in a new way, understanding how different sections of the school community experience time and how that relates to the desired change they hope to make in their system.

3.3 Summary

This chapter explored the key characteristics of a complex system. Importantly, we have developed a framework for understanding a Complex Adaptive System, in educational settings. System leaders now understand the importance of feedback (amplification and regulation); self-organisation through the use of weight of interaction, which creates network shapes; boundaries, especially perceived boundaries in the form of culture; the relativity of time; and, of most interest, emergence. These five concepts help to develop a complexity approach, which can be applied to educational settings. For systems leaders, this complexity approach allows them to recognise what is happening the present system but it does not explain what a system leader needs to do. This is because the first challenge is often simply to understand and define the complex system you want to engage with. By knowing this system leaders can now turn to a second aspect of understanding the complexity of their systems: how energy flows in their educational setting. The next chapter explores the energy needed in systems.

Notes

1 https://www.nobelprize.org/prizes/physics/2021/popular-information/
2 Roberts (2020).
3 I have often found that the process of emergence in schools creates new activities that generate excitement and are very hard for the system to resist, as they come from within, rather being imposed externally.

4 Energy in schools

When I think about the first day of term, there is often a buzz of conversation and laughter as staff and students catch up after their holidays, generating energy and enthusiasm. They feel refreshed and ready for the academic year. Significant events and changes are acknowledged and discussed, including the fact that some students have grown bigger, taller or (in some cases!) hairier. Our understanding of a Complex Adaptive System tells us that these conversations amplify the connections across different networks, shaping and re-forming them into self-organising networks. There is also excitement as students and staff form boundaries, deciding who is included and excluded from their groups. The implicit group boundaries that emerge dictate the school's culture independently of any one network or relationship.

The complexity framework outlined in Chapter 3 gave us a way to identify and understand this socially complex adaptive system using the concepts of feedback (amplification and regulation), self-organisation, emergence, boundaries and time. However, the system also requires energy; a system needs forms of energy to interconnect and thus create interdependencies. For example, photosynthesis (energy from the sun) allows plants to grow. Electricity provides energy for the mobile phone and laptop to work. What provides energy in socially complex adaptive systems such as schools? This chapter will seek to provide an answer.

For system leaders in socially complex systems, it is important to recognise and understand their system's energy dynamics to effect sustainable change. But while a system's energy source is often clear and explicit in the natural sciences (e.g., sunlight, water, air and food), it is much less apparent in the social and educational sciences. We might intuitively feel when a social system is building energy – the excitement of a reward or recognition, for example, or the nervous standstill before trouble at the school gate – but it is much harder to identify, define and quantify this form of system energy.

What generates energy in schools? To clarify things, we will consider three types of social energy we have already touched on: attention, information and money (see Figure 4.1).

I selected these three forms of system energy because they help explain why schools can maintain or grow certain aspects of their complex adaptive system

Figure 4.1 Social energy – attention, information and money.

while other features decline or disappear. Part of the challenge for system leaders is recognising, engaging and channelling the energy in schools. To think big, leaders must amplify the aspects they want to nurture. To think differently, they must understand how to harness social energy to create emergent features that expand a network's creativity. This chapter explores all three types of social energy – attention, information and money – in depth. Let us start with attention.

4.1 Attention

Tests on rapid eye movement show that our focus is surprisingly fleeting without a specific visual to hold our attention, with reaction times ranging from 14 milliseconds to 37 milliseconds (Mahon, Clarke and Hunt, 2018). In other words, attention can be a scarce commodity. I first came to the conclusion that attention is a form of social energy in systems while I read *The Attention Economy* (Davenport and Beck, 2001), as the authors suggested this would be vital to the development of future technologies.[1] Attention is a vital form of energy in social systems. Social Media and other technological systems have developed sophisticated ways to capture and maintain our attention. Think how often you look at your mobile device and how long you spend on various apps; this is by design. Yet, like the concept of time, that of 'attention' is often absent from leadership theory, and educational leadership in particular.

The Cambridge Dictionary defines attention as: notice, thought or interest, for example, to watch listen to, think about something or someone carefully or with interest. For this book's purposes, I define attention as the ability to combine focus and concentration. We will consider how schools and system leaders can utilise focus and concentration within their social systems. Consider a typical school day: how much can you genuinely give your full attention to? It is clear that attention is always in high demand, with staff constantly required to attend meetings, reply to emails and engage with students and parents. Therefore, the fundamental challenge for system leaders is focusing the people that matter on the interactions that matter. Given the myriad competing demands for attention, directing, channelling and retaining attention is vital to changing complex social systems. However, several factors play a role in shaping a system's attentional energy, as will be explored below.

4.1.1 Organisational focus

Similar to individual focus, organisational focus refers to an organisation's ability to maintain collective attention on a particular topic or overarching system feature. In the educational system, the challenge lies in maintaining a school's focus as waves of new initiatives crash on the collective shorelines of leadership teams' and staff thinking. The "new" often compels school leaders to jump from one programme or initiative to another as each new initiative seeks to capture their attention with the promise of making things ever more efficient or effective.

For example, imagine a school implementing a mental health programme to reduce teacher stress and burnout alongside a racial equity program to raise awareness of marginalisation of particular students and how they disproportionality achieve lower educational attainment over their time in the school. Both initiatives require system leaders' attention. If the attention flow allows the organisational focus to recognise both, this is an advantageous to the system's ability to cope. However, if the organisational focus is limited, then there is a decision as to which will receive the focus of the organisation. At worst, there will be a drift away from one or both initiatives, which demonstrates the school's finite and exhaustible attention reservoir is running low, indicating that other system priorities are dominating organisational focus.

Loss of focus may come from an internal challenge such as, "we care about racial equity, but we are more concerned about teacher burnout right now". Alternatively, it may derive from external pressure, such as "we care about racial equity *and* teacher burnout, but due to the upcoming school inspection, our current leadership focus is on improving grades". The net result is the same either way: the school loses focus on issues it claims to value.

Such loss of organisational focus undermines system leaders' ability to implement change. For example, if an organisation tries to implement too many things simultaneously, the cognitive overload diffuses its network's attention, and focus is lost. This is often seen during a crisis, when leaders want to change multiple system aspects at once but see them in isolation, implementing numerous concurrent initiatives that ultimately compete for leaders' focus and staff attention. A school can lose organisational focus if it tries to add too many new components, for example, social and emotional learning, mental health and well-being, mindfulness or stress management. Managers often seek to implement 'quick wins' driven by a school improvement agenda. The consequence of overloading organisational attention is that school leaders have no capacity left for studying the inter-initiative interactions. As a result, a way to manage attention overload is for school leaders to appoint champions or ambassadors for initiatives (demonstrating intent but without maintaining organisational focus) or institute a ceremonial day, week or month when attention is temporarily focused but rarely sustained as the next day, week or month then requires everyone to focus on that instead. Even if schools *do* maintain their organisational focus on a vision or value, a second competence is required: concentration.

4.1.2 Organisational concentration

With so many system aspects clamouring for system leaders' attention, knowing what to focus on is vital. Moreover, system leaders must also know how *long* they can concentrate on the things capturing their focus, which links to the perception of time. The many educational fads and fashions that pass through schools snare system members' focus, but how long do they have when they have the full concentration of the school before this wanes over time? I remember walking through a school where enormous keys hung over the corridors, but when I asked what the display was for, every staff member replied that it "was something the previous head did several years ago". Thus, the initiative's remnants remained but not the concentration.

Schools are bombarded with new ideas, processes and collaborative approaches in the yearly education cycle, but only some capture their focus, with even fewer their concentration. The reasons vary; some issues are more emotionally compelling, for example, dealing with racism, equity and disproportionality. Others may be necessary, such as addressing teacher burnout. But whatever they choose, system leaders must ask the fundamental question, "How do I galvanise networks to maintain *overall* organisational concentration on this issue, not just that of an individual or small group?" Bounded staff may naturally concentrate on a particular aspect because they are passionate about instigating change by the very fact there is a shared concern. Alternatively, some aspects of schooling are essential yet may not get the concentration required. A classic example is all staff being aware of a mandatory issue such as safeguarding;[2] some staff will not concentrate on the information provided, assuming the training is able to hold staff's attention because they have heard it before and now no longer concentrate on the information being provided.

To address this, system leaders must understand how to use feedback to maintain and amplify concentration levels. A school's ability to concentrate is crucial for avoiding the managerial temptation of implementing 'shiny new things'. These pique interest because they are novel and exciting but draw focus and attention away from the school's existing initiatives or interventions. By thinking differently, system leaders understand that implementing and sustaining system change depends on maintaining organisational concentration.

Networked concentration thus increases an organisation's ability to maintain focus on a particular systems-change issue. However, it can be particularly challenging for schools to sustain given the various institutional, community and political demands on them, that is, ensuring salaries are paid, collecting evidence for school inspections, and so forth. As attractive as individual leadership appears, it risks embodying the organisation's concentration in a single leader as an 'expert' or charismatic ambassador. While the leader's passion and commitment can be powerfully motivating, this strategy places all the organisation's 'concentration eggs' in one basket. If that individual burns out or moves on, they leave a gaping hole. Organisational concentration on that issue is then lost or suspended as the networks wait to see the new school leader's agenda and thus where attention will go.

Boredom is one way in which organisational focus and organisational concentration can drift. For example, during school meetings which routinely become simply cascading information as opposed to engaging staff, drift will start to creep as those in the network realise that communication is one-way and there are quicker ways to access the information. Alternatively, school INSET training, when all staff come together, is another example of when loss of staff concentration can occur. While concentration may be high on the day the charismatic, highly motivational speaker presents, staff attention drops dramatically once the students return to school, as their attention shifts to the routines and rituals of the school day. The annual INSET rarely retains the staff's concentration and needs ongoing collective (network) reinforcement. System leaders must identify how their networks can ensure such concentration levels are not one-offs.

4.1.3 Experiential focus

System leaders' ability to use attention depends on how effectively they can build and channel it. The easiest way to amplify attention is to find others who are already interested in the same topic, which magnifies interest through connection, that is, the weight of interaction. Potential bounded actors may be relatively easy to identify for topics that affect everybody. For example, finding staff and pupils interested in protecting the environment may be relatively straightforward, since it is a community issue relevant to all school members and exposure to the 'problem' is relatively equal. In contrast, fewer people may be interested in addressing the sexual harassment of girls in a school since it can be perceived is a minority issue affecting only a subset of community members. Although many school members might consider it an important topic, they may not want to give attention to it as they do not have experience, for example, male staff.

Therefore, system leaders must first recognise how to generate and focus attention. One option is to create a shared experience. For example, if litter or overflowing bins are an issue, system leaders can create a shared experience to direct and focus group attention, for example, a school tidy day on a weekly or monthly basis involve the students and staff. Rather than using sanctions or punishments against such undesired outcomes, a systems leader could provide a fun, practical and educational way to approach the issue by organising a regular slot where staff and students come together to sort items that can be recycled and those that can't. To increase focus and attention, house or class points could be awarded for each type of item found and correctly disposed of. In this way, the systems leader creates a collaboratively fun and empowering shared experience in addressing an issue by allowing others to be involved and to connect.[3]

However, a school's litter problem is visible to all members and collectively experienced, while only a minority of members experience sexual harassment. Members of the school community may be aware that girls are being sexually harassed, but attention to the problem is not the same as attention to the solution. The experience instantly grabs attention, and for those that have this experience, they will seek to focus others in the school to gain support in changing the situation. Therefore, an issue which affects a minority must be articulated, which in itself can be challenging; that is, articulating an experience into other forms, for example, writing or drawings, does not capture the reasons why the experience has become such a focal point. At a systems level before leaders can move towards solutions, recognising how a system creates those experiences is essential. For example. while a school might focus on male students' behaviour to address the problem, this form of solution tries to solve a systems issue by targeting individuals or a single group. It thus fails to recognise that the school's community is greater than the groups within, which means the problem cannot be 'fixed' by modifying one component, in this case a group, independently of other features, such as policy, referrals and interventions. The temptation to do so shows the power of Taylorism, which is what needs to be resisted by system leaders.

Our experience of an issue may also depend on our sensory immersion; the more senses engaged by an experience, the greater attention we give it. Think about 'death by PowerPoint' presentation, where low sensory engagement yields low attention! In addition, the greater the number of school members immersed in the experience, the more likely the issue will attract attention. Conversely, the fewer people affected, the less attention the issue attracts. Hence, school system leaders must channel attention to generate adequate focus on the topic of concern. Furthermore, they must develop ways to concentrate attention and sustain an understanding of what is happening in the system.

4.1.4 Emotions as signs of attention capture

Emotions are potent focusers of attention, which is why emotional 'hooks' are so powerful. The word 'emotion' derives from the Latin word *emovere*, meaning "to move, move out or move through". Thus, an emotion is essentially movement, and to be moved requires our attention on the thing(s) that move us. But for most people, systems are rarely emotionally interesting – they are more emotionally engaged by the problems or solutions systems create.

Table 4.1 The Big Six Emotions

Joy	Fear	Sadness
Disgust	Anger	Surprise

I really value the work Dr Daniel Ekman,[4] who has done extensive study on how we recognise emotions across cultures (2003). His work (Ekman and Wallace, 2003) identified the big six emotions – see Table 4.1 – and their corresponding facial expressions. Importantly, from Ekman's research the big six are recognised across cultures; so whether we are Massai tribespersons near the African Great Lakes or a New Yorker in Manhattan, we will recognise these emotional expressions in each other. Emotions can also be described in terms of intensity; I can be frustrated or apoplectic with rage, both describe the emotion of anger but with different intensities. Essentially, any one of the big six means that our attention has been engaged; when more than one is aroused our attention is even more focused.

When seeking change in a school's system, system leaders need to consider which emotions hold the school community's attention on the issue at stake. For example, do they feel sad about the amount of litter or disgusted that the bins are overflowing? There is a temptation to ignore emotional aspects in favour of the mechanics of change, yet this often ignores the school's culture – the emotional boundaries of what *is* and *is not* acceptable. By recognising the emotions arising with system change, system leaders can identify and engage emergent emotional attention in a system.

I once worked with a school where sexual harassment of female students was prevalent, and female students felt real anger about the daily behaviour of male students they had to tolerate. They also felt frustration about the staff's lack of action (and, by extension, their lack of attention) on the issue. Conversely, the male students I engaged with thought it was okay to touch girls inappropriately, seeing it as a bit of fun and harmless joking around. Not only did they believe such behaviour was acceptable, but the absence of staff attention to the issue endorsed it by default.[5]

For system leaders, channelling attention through recognising and articulating emotions is thus vital to thinking big and thinking differently. System leaders must understand how to engage with existing networks and their emotional feedback loops, recognise what emotions are getting attention and whether these are the ones which will help bring about the system change they need to enact.

4.1.5 *Organisational noise*

Focus and concentration combine to generate attention in systems. However, if multiple system activities require attention, the limits of individual and organisational attention may be reached. We can focus on only so many things at once, with research suggesting between five and nine at any time (Miller, 1956). Therefore, system leaders must recognise that attentional overload will cause their team's or system's change initiative to lose concentration as they are required to focus on more and more aspects of the system.

Attention overload creates organisational noise, leading to an inability to differentiate and attend to a specific issue or system feature. Organisational Noise for our purposes will be defined as "the amount of information which overloads the system to the point it becomes indiscernible"; as I differentiate between organisational noise and how Kahneman, Sibony and Sunstein (2021) use the term 'noise' in regard to the "the unwanted variability in judgements that should ideally be identical" (2021, p. 21). In effect, organisational noise makes it difficult to focus, let alone concentrate, as is often the case when major systems change is implemented so rapidly that no one person or team can focus on all the changes occurring. This hinders system leaders' ability to give attention to the change they want to see as the organisational noise overloads the networks and individuals tasked with making this happen.

Increased organisational noise from newer, more exciting initiatives captures interest but can exhaust a school's finite reservoir of attention. For example, consider the sheer number of emotional health and well-being initiatives that schools could apply compared to how many they actually deliver; in addition, staff faced with multiple new initiatives have to decide where to put their attention. This can be especially challenging if there are contradictions between the initiatives which make it difficult to understand how they interconnect.

Organisational noise and boredom can stagnate attention as a form of system energy. As information becomes repetitive, attention can drift and dissipate. This can be seen in schools that deliver the same INSET training year after year, based on the same PowerPoint slides and exercises. Staff may be highly attentive in the first year but are significantly less engaged by the fourth, when the content has lost its novelty and attraction. Not only have I seen staff leave the room because the information no longer holds their attention, but a head teacher once praised me because no one walked out during the INSET session I delivered to the school's staff! I had kept their attention.

Another sure-fire way of killing attention is an unengaging delivery format, which dampens focus and concentration. In another school, I had a member of the staff say I had done a great job as he had fallen asleep only once. Staff attention is definitely a finite, precious resource! Furthermore, a classic example of draining system energy as attention is the poorly chaired meeting whose attendees wonder what its point is, often reflected in reduced attendance over time because the meeting fails to hold people's attention. In this case, the meeting itself has become part of the school's organisational noise, despite what was the best of intentions.

However, organisational noise cannot be completely excluded and is always present in schools. The system leader's goal is not to eliminate it but to recognise how they can work with it to facilitate, nurture and sustain the emergence they seek.

4.1.6 Attentional redundancy

Attentional redundancy is the ability to recognise in the educational setting aspects of the system which retain attention, are no longer necessary or able to hold attention. Objects, people, teams and projects all have their moments, but then there is a point at which the system needs to let go or refocus its attention. This can be the case when a feature if the system such as staff talking about a previous initiative which has long since ceased to be in effect still keeps their attention. The challenge of the system leader is to shift focus and concentration away from the features of the system which are redundant, yet still keep attention and allow it to flow into the new system change. This is easier said than done, especially where staff have had the experience, and emotional connection of, for example, an old school leader who was amazing and used to do x, y and z. Alternatively, there can be talk about the old days, such as how bad student behaviour was and how new staff don't know what things were like before. Either way, there is a danger that attention is being made redundant by being used on stories and experiences which are no longer relevant to the present system state. For system leaders, attention is a form of system energy; the skill is in utilizing focus and concentration to enable the change they want to see in their school and communities.

4.2 Information

This section refers to information as *the way a system's knowledge is explained*, which can be subdivided into *explicit* and *implicit* information, drawing on the insightful work of Nonaka and Takeuchi (1995). The distinction they make helps us to understand both forms of information, as well as how implicit and explicit information can be transformed from one type into the other, which is vital for system leaders to recognize. Let us begin with explicit information.

4.2.1 Explicit information

Explicit information is clearly stated and complete. A school visitor will often encounter explicit information quite quickly – for example, a picture of all the staff or students, a school trophy case or a behaviour chart displayed in the corridor. Moreover, explicit information is often in text form, such as written statements about the school community. Other forms of explicit information include policies, processes and organisational outcomes, which can take the form of reports and documents. Since explicit information offers greater transferability between the writer and the reader, explicit information transferred through the system is assumed to be accurate based on a shared understanding of the writer's intentions. The critical question, however, is how much it holds people's attention. Hence, some policies 'are left in the drawer' and 'get reviewed once a year'. While explicit information's content is important, the time spent engaging with it relates to what is happening in other parts of the system.

Action plans are another form of explicit information, often attracting and dominating attention because of their visual RAG (red, amber, green) systems. Action plans use diagrams, flow charts and graphs to make a team's specific goals and intentions explicit as clearly, comprehensibly and accessibly as possible. However, the authors of explicit information in schools rarely check whether their audience has received and understood their message, resulting in a low interaction weight. Indeed, the (in) accessibility of explicit information often reflects its creators' intentions, that is, the use of jargon (boundary formation and maintenance) and educational acronyms (shorthand for those know who know and a barrier to those who don't). The power of acronyms is their ability to define in-group behavior, and can be excluded from the conversation.

The challenge for system leaders is to see explicit language with new eyes. This can involve testing explicit knowledge among different school groups to see if its meaning is shared or exclusive or seeking external stakeholders' views (e.g., parents, charity or business partners, or the wider community). It is critical to recognise that the familiarity of explicit information can often lead to complacency of assumed meaning if it has been present in the system long enough that people no longer question it.

Explicit information is often used to evidence progress, change or failure, as inspection regimes and school leadership theories have created the perception that it is the most legitimate form of information. Technology has partly helped perpetuate this dominance as inspection regimes often use it to justify courses of action. But system leaders must recognise that explicit information is often contextualised by implicit information, to which we will now turn our attention.

4.2.2 Implicit Information

Implicit information is ubiquitous in schools. Unlike explicit information, it is not directly stated but can be inferred through hints and clues. Even during teacher training on the first day of term, implicit information is evident in who sits with whom, what they discuss and when (and to whom) hugs and smiles are given. Similarly, students share implicit information in how they treat each other and behave. Implicit information is communicated more subtly than explicit information via behavioural nuances, voice tone, body language, facial expressions or informal rituals. As such, implicit information is often found in the unsaid.

Since implicit information signals what is socially acceptable and unacceptable, system leaders in socially complex adaptive systems must recognise how such information is exchanged within and between groups. In the context of schools, implicit information is generated by system leaders and by the rituals, norms and expectations of different 'tribes' within the school community. For example, tribal behaviour might be seen in how the maths department communicates with the PE department or how science teachers congregate around the coffee machine. These are all social cues embedded in implicit information. Having sat in many staff canteens for lunch, I am always fascinated by its display of tribal behaviours, that is, where an individual or group can sit and what the expected greeting or comment is in the adult-owned space.

The key point for system leaders is to recognise what norm the system perpetuates, the expected behaviours and the accompanying perceptions. It always surprises me how few opportunities there are for educationists to come together simply to discuss a topic and see what emerges in the room. At other points, what is believed to be a common norm can quickly give way to a spectrum of opinions, while in other cases, a majority consensus means few will openly disagree. System leaders must apply the complexity approach to identify what a system's implicit information is regulating, and how it amplifies the weight of interactions also carries implicit information with regard to norms, rituals and beliefs.

Implicit information resides within a school's culture, which generates the system's regularity, that is, the interactions with which staff and young people become familiar with regularity. A systems leader recognises that a system is not shaped by "the way we do things around here", as Tuckman and Jensen defined classroom culture in 1977, but rather by the totality of interactions occurring within a social network. Though not as punchy as Tuckman and Jensen's definition, oversimplifying culture undermines how challenging it can be to change.

Implicit information's power lies in how quickly it can grab our attention – because we feel it viscerally with our senses, make judgements from it and normalise because of it. Excitement or fatigue in meetings indicates whether the information is worthy of attention. Implicit information reinforces boundary formation and maintenance in schools, that is, "what we don't do around here", or who keeps within a perceived 'tribe'. At other points, implicit information may be in the yearning for change, for greater aspiration which has not yet been bounded or become a network; the frustration is not with the "new" but with the lack of opportunity to think big and differently.

4.3 Money

4.3.1 Money as energy

School funding is often a hot political topic, generating fierce controversy about how to ensure educational systems are adequately funded to achieve the best educational outcomes. In the UK, a simple view is that schools funded via the government (state schools) have an allocated budget, whereas fee-charging schools (private schools) depend on the number of places they fill. Together, they form the basis of the UK's educational eco-system.

Understanding how money forms part of the social energy in socially complex adaptive systems requires system leaders to expand the concept of money. School funding is a means for schools to acquire the resources necessary to meet their functional needs. However, the flow of money into schools has changed significantly in the last 20 years, with schools expected to have greater financial independence and accountability despite continued funding through the Department for Education (DfE) in England.

On its own, money has no inherent value – it is simply piles of paper or digits on a screen – it is the representation of value. But as a form of energy, it can be exchanged for resources that can hold information and attention in a school. These include explicit-information resources, such as books and training materials, and implicit-information resources, such as inviting a guest speaker to talk to students about diversity and mental health. As a form of social energy, money thus has the power to transform resources, gain information and attract attention. Consequently, systems leader need to recognise how money flows through their system in similar ways to attention and information.

Numerous reports highlight how valuable education is to young people's life chances. Yet the price of something does not indicate how money is used as a form of social energy. For example, sending a child to a private boarding school in England such as Eton can cost up to £47,000 per year, whereas placing a child in a Youth Offending Institution (a prison for under 18s in England and Wales) costs £119,000 per year, per child in 2021 (UK Parliament, Written Questions, 19 July 2021). Just consider that for a moment: it costs over twice as much to send a child to a Youth Offending Institution than to Eton, yet the consequences are diametrically opposed! Likewise, it is estimated that exclusion from school will, on average, cost society an additional £370,000 per excluded child's lifetime[6] (via lost taxation due to reduced future earnings, increased benefit pay-outs, higher healthcare costs and a greater likelihood of prison time). Thus, although exclusion costs nothing for a school, the costs to our *system* are substantial. Moreover, as a form of social energy, there is no direct relationship between what schools do with money and the educational benefits gained. Hence, money may be a crude system measure, particularly as budgets contribute to system's deconstruction.

For system leaders, it is vital to understand how money can combine with attention and information to inject energy towards system change. Purchasing a resource (e.g., a new mental health programme) may be costly, but the expense may also ensure a concentrated focus on its success. Therefore, money and attention can, in some cases, interact as a form of social energy. In other, an equally expensive purchase (e.g., electronic tablets) does not attract teachers' attention or impact their teaching style in the same way. Therefore, the resource's expense is less noticeable. Hence, system leaders must understand money's transformative effect and influence on aspects of the system they seek to change.

4.3.2 Money and the conversion into system resources

From a school perspective, money as system energy can be converted into resources such as INSET training, both the cost of staff attending as well as having external speakers. Indeed, it is fascinating to see how much system leaders spend on staff training when they think about money as a form of energy. Such training costs include fixed venue costs – usually the school's assembly hall – and variable costs, such the external speakers and staff attendance on the day. However, the system's energy types also combine in these moments. For example, an external speaker's ability to hold the staff's attention is crucial to how successfully the information is received; its inherent value may not be enough to command attention if delivered via 100 PowerPoint slides!

The converse is also true, with schools spending huge sums on speakers who provide very little information but are charismatic and compelling. However, I have always been interested in how INSET can provide new information and explore perspective sharing. Moreover, there is potential to allow staff to share their own meaning-making within their collective experience in an INSET session, enabling networking and the emergence of new system behaviours. However, educational systems normalise INSET's rituals and costs rather than recognising money as a form of system energy that could be used to reshape it.

One of the most interesting aspects of money as systemic energy is the ability to devolve budgets to other parts of the system. Sharing or devolving money to a particular system feature signifies the importance a school places on it. However, financing a system aspect as a one-off is not as powerful as financing it regularly, since one-off financing may be tokenistic, whereas regular financing can increase the weight of interaction and signify trust for those involved. Often, schools allocate money as a one-off cost, hoping it will be within budget and achieve a range of system changes. Many school initiatives I have worked on received funding for starting costs but fell foul of a presumption that the initiative would self-sustain once up and running on attention and information. However, the initial funding rarely provides the energy needed for an initiative to survive in a system as complex as a school.

Indeed, initiating change is often more challenging than initially thought by those involved, depending on how ready and willing the system is. But readiness and willingness do not always go hand in hand. Hence, system leaders must recognise that money as an energy source is transferable and transformative, signalling levels of trust in the system and amplifying collaboration with children, young people, parents or staff. For example, allocating a student council budget creates an opportunity for them to transform ideas into resources or new experiences. The school demonstrates trust in the student council's decision-making and allows it to develop artefacts (create new objects imbued with meaning through collaboration) and refine ideas and experiences. Otherwise, the tokenism comes when school activities can no longer be done on zero budget, reducing the quality of the other two forms of energy – information and attention.

These three forms of energy are also interrelated. For example, there is an inherent cost to asking staff and students to give their attention to something.

Therefore, seeking to instigate system change via a meeting, discussion or group setting often involves costs that are rarely acknowledged. In my own research exploring system leadership with a group of staff, I found it interesting to observe discussions about the most appropriate time to host additional staff training and the inherent tensions involved in balancing money, attention and information considerations. Their discussion varied between hosting a twilight session (an after-school session) that would attract staff willing to prioritise the session above their other duties and a formal INSET session during school hours that would optimise attendance. Since twilight sessions are voluntary, the school leadership saw this as a cheap option that would also reveal which staff were willing, curious and motivated enough to give up their time to attend the session. However, as they ultimately sought a meshed-network effect, the leadership team recognised that the system change they sought required the majority of staff to participate – most likely achieved by adding the training to the school's INSET sessions. This option would also signify the importance the senior leadership team placed on this information. INSET's costs mean all staff are expected to attend, meaning that such a session had a high value (and cost) to the school. However, the school INSET calendar had been booked a year in advance, so the first available INSET slot was in 18 months. From a system leadership perspective, the school's time and expense were perceived as boundaries, presenting them with a dilemma: should they start small and cheap now with twilight sessions (quicker and at a lower cost, but yielding less attention/information) or wait to start bigger but at a greater cost (slow and more expensive to implement, but yielding greater attention/information)? In the end, they decided to meet again to develop an action plan for delivering their desired change. Unfortunately, that meeting never happened; thus, the cost of implementation became a one-off loss to the school. As they did not factor the cost of finding time to meet again into their planning, they lost focus and failed to share the information to enable system change.

4.4 Reflection on system energy

While applying a complex adaptive systems framework to schools identifies its key system features, we can explain those features' dynamics only by identifying the system's energy forms and flow. Considered separately, each energy form – attention, information and money – helps identify a different system dynamic. In combination, however, they show system leaders how a system might amplify, regulate or negate change in the system they seek to modify. System leaders' skill thus lies in determining how best to harness the system's social energy to facilitate the emergence of a new state that meets their school community's needs and in diverting system energy away from undesired features to cut through the organisational noise or redirect redundant attention. Importantly, system energy provides a way for system leaders to understand that 'no feedback is feedback'; the absence of attention, information and money is feedback in itself.

Tracking the *absence* of system change was one of the biggest challenges I faced as a professional and a researcher, as inaction preserves the status quo. This chapter helps leaders be more confident and capable of thinking big and thinking differently by enabling them to recognise the importance of social energy and its power in schools.

Notes

1. Look at how much time you have spent on your mobile phone this week to see how right they were.
2. Safeguarding is a mandatory requirement as per the Children's Act 1989, and the Education Act 2002, to keep children safe from abuse and look after their emotional wellbeing.
3. During my secondary school, I was asked by the deputy head teacher to pick all the rubbish in the playground. I really resented being the only one asked to do. Whereas, my daughter is a keen protector of the environment and has made me walk behind with a bag as she has picked up litter. Although the action is the same the experience and emotional connection are totally different.
4. Dr Paul Ekman's work is extensive in this area, so I have referenced the first book I read if readers want to begin to explore this area more.
5. The school went on to address the problem via a combination of restorative practice, awareness workshops, better reporting of incidents and a policy review.
6. https://www.prospectmagazine.co.uk/politics/cost-of-excluding-a-child-public-money

5 Understanding your system

Previous chapters built a way of engaging, analysing and considering schools as complex adaptive systems. This chapter looks at how to apply these ideas to schools as complex social systems: how to recognise where you are in your system, what we can call positionality. We then turn to forms of power that are possible in a complex adaptive system before we understand the range of stakeholders involved in educational settings. We will then explore how you can get to know your system via mental and physical maps and identify how the system behaves. This will enable you to recognise your system's present state and how it evolved. Let us begin with recognising our position in the system.

5.1 Positionality

The term 'positionality' is in reference to the position we may take on a topic; for example, should all schools reduce the summer holiday and extend the Christmas holidays? The question at first appears as a simple yes or no. But there are other positions that could be taken, for example, extend the half-term holidays. This would be a different position; a fourth position would be to have fewer holidays but shorten the school day. The key point here is that I not only have an opinion, but I recognise that this opinion is part of a constellation of other options. I may take a position because I agree with it (which is usually the case), or I may take a different position to explore other ways of thinking, alternatively to understand why that opinion is valid for those that agree. We will explore the importance for system leaders in knowing their position; that is, your positionality is crucial, as we shall see.

5.1.1 Role position

The most obvious form of positionality is the positions within school organisations which are understood as functional roles – the role that specifies particular duties and requirements, for example, a lunchtime supervisor, teaching assistant, teacher, janitor, year-group head, deputy head, head teacher (School Administrator in the USA) and so forth. However, such roles can also create responsibility and accountability that in theory demarcate clear boundaries, creating the perception that the role-holder exclusively manages those responsibilities and other members of staff do not need to be involved. Furthermore, organisational hierarchy can exacerbate such role-specific accountability; the higher up a role is, the more responsibility and accountability are presumed to accompany it. So, the position in the hierarchy is known to others in the educational settings by role, title and responsibilities. For example, in English Schools the term head teacher is used for the top of the hierarchy, followed by deputy-head; such titles make clear the position. But what about viewing schools through the lens of complex adaptive systems; how do we our position and that of others?

5.1.2 Network position

A complex adaptive system perspective provides an alternative approach, focusing on the network shapes a system leader belongs to within a school rather than on their functional role. Firstly, different network shapes explain the kinds of cross-school interactions a system's leaders are engaged in. Secondly, a network's shape determines how a system leader will be most likely to behave. For example, a hub-and-spoke network may involve a constant stream of information to members of each 'spoke', which can lead to a command-and-control form of behaviour. In contrast, a loose network may increase the need to check in with colleagues as information is shared and communicated through multiple people. Conversely, while a teachers WhatsApp group may be a highly meshed network, the system leader may receive the same information simultaneously – leading the group to view them as an equal. Hence, recognising the shape of the networks that system leaders belong to is key to recognising one's own position. This position will change depending on both the types of networks we belong to and on when the networks themselves change shape, due to the weight of interaction.

5.1.3 Position to amplify and regulate

In addition, to understand our position in a system we must recognise what we amplify and what we regulate. Imagine a new school corridor policy requiring students to walk on a particular side of the corridors, for example. The policy's success would depend on the staff acting as (*a*) amplifiers, for example, monitoring students' compliance during breaks and classroom transitions, and (*b*) regulators, for example, reminding students (and other staff members) to walk on the right side of the corridor to maintain efficient flow. Knowing what we amplify and regulate is vital in recognising our position in the system. Who – and what – a school's networks support reveals the particular messages we amplify and, thus, their importance. Likewise, staff who continuously shoot down new ideas may already feel overloaded are seeking to regulate the present rather than amplify the future.

5.2 The power of positionality

Recognising who holds power in the system is a crucial aspect of systems leadership, though not as straightforward as it might seem. Most hierarchical school structures presume that those at the top hold more power than those at the bottom. From a systems perspective, however, participants hold different *types* of power capable of affecting the system's behaviour. In identifying the types of power this may also help to define what *power* is. Therefore, I will suggest that power comprises four main categories: the power to attract, maintain, reject or opt-out. We can use this quartet of power types to explore why understanding school systems requires us to recognise our and others' positions in the system and what forms of power are in play. Let us explore each one in turn.

5.2.1 The power to attract

The power to attract can take various forms. Firstly, the power to instigate or catalyse a new idea attracts bounded actors to a new energy source in the system. When a new head teacher joins a school, for example, they bring different ideas and experiences, attracting actors and networks that begin amplifying change in the system. However, amplification may come from sources other than senior leaders, for example, teachers interested in alternative pedagogy. The key for systems leaders is identifying where the amplification originates, especially since amplification can show where disharmony and conflict may arise. For example, a conflict between two staff members in one secondary school I worked in had been amplified so much that it divided the staffroom into two opposing camps. The cause of that conflict was between the two staff yet their power to attract other members of staff to their side was the catalyst for the division. Staff were literally forced to pick a position.

5.2.2 The power to maintain

A second feature of systems power is the ability to maintain, which is closely related to the ability to regulate. Rather than rejecting the specific change per se, members of the school community may often resist system change because they fear the unknown and what it might mean for them; maintaining the familiar is a powerful force in schools. Once a particular way of working becomes ritualised, it develops a self-perpetuating web of co-dependent connections. School community members then compare the perceived boundary of 'what is' to the unknown of 'what could be', causing discomfort. The energy to maintain the status quo is part of how the system self-regulates, which can be perceived as familiar. For example, the ritual familiarity of school detention supports its continuation, despite the possibility of more constructive uses of time and place to instigate meaningful change with students. Even providing an evidence base on why detention is not effective can undermine teachers, staff and students' familiarity and dependency on the school detention process. The ability to maintain is a position which holds power, especially in the face of the need to change to create new benefits in the educational setting.

5.2.3 The power to reject

A system's ability to reject is closely linked to its power to maintain, since rejecting change may also preserve the school's current system. Therefore, the power to reject prevents unwelcome fads as well as innovation from entering the system. This power is often in direct conflict with amplification; as some school members seek to bring about change, others reject what is happening but do not necessarily want to maintain the status quo. For example, the lunchtime supervisors in one school I worked in rejected the introduction of Peer Mediators, the ability for children to use dialogue to resolve low-level peer disputes, which they perceived as taking away their power in the playground. Nevertheless, they also wanted better student behaviour during the lunch break, so they were not happy to maintain the current playgroup behaviour. This created a tension between wanting change but rejecting ways in which this could happen. The power to reject may mean that others have to work out someone's position as they do not state their position. For sytem leaders, the power of rejection can be especially challenging when members of the school community do not explicitly state members of the school community are rejecting something, which leads to our final form of power, the power to opt-out.

5.2.4 The power to opt-out

The power to opt-out of the system is often highly underrated; not engaging can be an act of passive resistance or rejection. For example, parents in one school who disagreed with the head teacher's handling of teacher/student conflict withdrew their children and changed schools, indicating that they did not feel they had the power to attract change or reject the present situation, and definitely did not want the present situation to be maintained either. Such parents perceived opting-out as their only option. When systems leaders look at power in socially complex systems such as schools, recognising an absence of feedback helps identify where the system is not engaging, leaving the question, "Is no feedback a form of feedback?"

5.3 Understanding power and positionality in my system

We have now explored four types of power, which enable us to define power as: "the ability to attract, maintain, reject or opt-out of systems". Positionality tells where we are in the system, but power and how it manifests helps to show what needs to happen to think differently about school systems change; hence, systems leaders must recognise who has power and what type(s) are being used. The power quartet shows that network actors who can use all four – attract, maintain, reject and opt-out – will be the most powerful in the system. Conversely, those most marginalised by the school change may be dissatisfied with the status quo but lack the energy to attract an alternative state or reject the current one. Thus, they opt out. This is where hierarchal leadership often makes the classic mistake of thinking that those against them must be the loudest voices of dissent, whereas they often quietly leave or disengage.

5.4 System stakeholders

In the business world, anyone with a share in the company can potentially influence it since they have exchanged their money (investment) for part of the business (equity). Therefore, the company's leaders must consider these shareholders' needs and opinions. However, stakeholders are a broader category of engagers and influencers than shareholders, comprising those with *any* interest or concern in an organisation or enterprise – and whose support is necessary for it to be successful. In short, a stakeholder can *affect* or *be affected by* the organisation in question. While it can thus be tempting to say everybody is a stakeholder, it is helpful to distinguish between stakeholder types.

We can now apply this to educational settings. For example, staff and students are two broad categories of a school's stakeholders. Parents are another, and can be subdivided into 'potential' and 'attached' parents – that is, those whose children might attend the school in the future and those with children currently at the school. From a systems leadership perspective, recognising different stakeholder types is essential for understanding who influences and is influenced by schools as complex systems. Recognising that such categorisation can create and maintain perceived boundaries between different groups within a school's community is also important.

Let us now identify a range of stakeholders in your school: staff, parents and students.

5.4.1 Staff

Although school staff are the most consistent part of the school community, systems leaders must be mindful that the generic label 'staff' hides the nuance of stakeholder types it encompasses, including administration, cleaning, support and teaching staff. Just as their roles and identities vary significantly, so will their needs, experiences, and perspectives in the system. Therefore, systems leaders must recognise staff sub-groups and implicit social groupings – often evident simply from where people tend to sit in the staff room, for example. I remember one primary school where the teaching assistants generally sat on the couch while the teachers sat at the table, with neither group crossing the perceived boundary. Such subdivisions represent important social and structural boundaries in the system, delineating each group's unique perspective.

Internal engagement of staff can be both exciting and frustrating. In one secondary school I worked with, staff enthusiastically brainstormed ideas about engaging students in various assemblies, curriculum activities and drop-down days (cross-curricular days) to encourage students towards greater ownership of their behaviour, generating an excellent range of proposals. However, they did not at any point speak to students or senior leaders about their ideas. Thus, they failed to engage different stakeholders, as a result, and frustratingly, they achieved little more than committing to a meeting to write an action plan. For system leaders, this highlights the importance of the creative potential of staff to generate emergent ideas which can be meaningful for their educational setting. However, they did not have the power to attract support and thus amplify the change they would have liked to see in their school.

5.4.2 Parents

Parental engagement is particularly interesting for schools. All schools must engage with the parents of potential students they wish to attract via their reputation, website or – most importantly – by word of mouth. Amplification of a school's favourable reputation can increase the number of parents recommending the school to one another. Likewise, amplification of a school's *unfavourable* reputation can endure, regardless of the school's current successes or achievements. In one school I worked in many years ago, the legacy of its poor reputation in the 1980s meant that parents sent their children there only when all other schools' places were full, even though the school's current teaching and pastoral support were excellent. In the end, the school resorted to changing its name.

Furthermore, schools also engage with current students' parents, although to varying degrees. At one end of the spectrum are parents who do not engage with the school at all, whose reasons may vary. For example, I remember one secondary school with low parental engagement due to the local factory's dominance as the town's major employer. Although parents fulfilled their legal requirement to send their children to school, they did not see education – and therefore school engagement – as beneficial in its own right. Equally, it became clear to me while working with second-generation West Indian parents in London that their experiences of education and racism created an uncomfortable tension. They wanted better educational opportunities for their children but did not trust educational professionals to understand their lived experiences. How system leaders use the weight of interaction to create network shapes with their students' parents can enhance levels of parental engagement.

5.4.3 Students

Perceptions of children and young people as school-community stakeholders are as varied as schools themselves. Some schools see children and young people as mere empty vessels to pour knowledge into and test their retention of it.[1] Others prioritise the creation of enriched experiences enabling children and young people to learn about themselves, others and the world around them. Ensuring that children and young people have a voice is crucial to how they are perceived as stakeholders in the school. For children and young people, opportunities such as vertical year groups allow them to connect with older or younger members of the school community. Rather than being confined solely to a single class or (horizontal) year group, such opportunities enable students to see how different students experience school.

Engaging with students as stakeholders can also mean engaging with the full range of students' school experiences, not just the 'average' experience. Students at the same school do not necessarily have the same experience. Some groups will have substantially different ones, including those whose first language is not English, those with special educational needs and/or disabilities, or those who are bored and disengaged with the school's educational process because they lack a motivational 'hook' to focus them.

By identifying and engaging with the full spectrum of student experiences, systems leaders are better informed to begin meeting their needs. For example, I spent four weeks with Year 6 students in one primary school discussing their concerns about starting secondary school. The transition from primary to secondary school can often be difficult. Their concerns ranged from leaving friends behind to getting to know multiple new teachers – concerns shared across different classes. The students came up with ways to stay connected and tips to help them navigate the challenges of year 7. When seeking to change the system, system leaders listening to students' concerns and experiences is be one way to see the school from the students' perspective.

5.4.4 Engaging with multiple system stakeholders

For systems leaders to fully understand their system, it is crucial that they engage with as many stakeholders as possible. I once supported a new head teacher in improving their school's relationship with the local community, since student behaviour was a major cause of concern. However, it became clear from engaging with the staff and parents that if the parents challenged a particular staff member and did not get what they wanted, they would simply approach another staff member to try to have the issue addressed their preferred way. Staff ended up actively undermining each other, since their lack of shared values enabled parents to play them off against each other. Consequently, students were unclear about the staff's behavioural expectations. Furthermore, the frequent parental complaints about other children reflected a lack of connection between parents as a group. From a systems leadership perspective, the analysis indicated multiple stakeholders acting as bounded agents, necessitating considerable time and energy in addressing their concerns and conflict. However, an external partner's fresh eyes and perspective can provide systems leaders with new system insights and approaches, especially when behaviours and norms are so habitual that they are no longer challenged. Importantly, multiple perspectives when embraced can help to understand why the school as a system is behaving the way it is and what is the potential for change from multiple perspectives.

5.4.5 Inviting an outside eye

As the above example shows, external partners' perspectives can thus be crucial in understanding how others see the school's behaviour as a system. Public-sector partners such as health professionals or police will have a particular perception of the school and their professional and organisational relationships within it. Working with 80–120 schools during my time in Local Authority, for example, I could immediately recognise which schools collaborated with a range of stakeholders, which schools were insular and defensive, and which schools actively undermined their stakeholder relationships. Being the outsider but working collaboratively allowed for different insights.

Where it is not always possible or necessary to have an outsider's eye, system leaders can use an alternative approach often used in the business world to investigate how an organisation's competitors or partners perceive it. In the education sector, this would involve gathering other schools' and external partners' opinions of your school. Why would this help? Because, despite the widespread assumption that parents decide which school to send their children based on League Tables and statistics, the school's reputation in the wider community is often much more important. A school's reputation in the wider community has a powerful and enduring influence on parental choices in the same way that brand association can dictate consumer choices more than a product's attributes. Identifying how a school is perceived thus sheds light on the wider issues, and the more choice is available in the community, the more a systems leader must be aware of how the school is perceived. Importantly, system leaders must be ready to hear different perspectives that do not conform to their view without rejecting the outsider's perception. Moreover, the value of outsider perspectives can be an alternative way to gain insight into their system.

5.5 Mapping your school as a complex adaptive system

How systems leaders perceive stakeholders and the features they use to identify different groups sheds light on how different community members behave. For example, Table 5.1 below shows six ways to group students.

How a system leader categorises school community members in Table 5.1 will determine the groups they belong to and their associated boundaries. Stakeholder engagement is thus crucial to understanding complex adaptive systems, helping to recognise different perspectives within the school community. If leaders assume that everyone in a generic category holds the same perspective, it may come as a surprise when certain groups push back against system change. Instead, understanding and engaging with different stakeholders enables systems leaders to hear, understand and integrate as-yet-unheard

Table 5.1 Student groupings based on twofold identifiers

Sex	Female	Male
Gender	Trans	Binary
Age	Chronological	Developmental
Race	White	Children of colour
Ability	Able-bodied	Disabled
Neurodiversity	Recognised	Unrecognised

voices and experiences. However, systems leaders in schools must avoid tokenistic stakeholder engagement with the school community.

5.5.1 Understanding the 'participation ladder' to engage your system

To help recognise such tokenistic engagement, Arnstien (1969) outlined an eight-rung participation typology she called the 'participation ladder', adapted here for a school setting (see Table 5.2, below).

We can then use Arnstein's Ladder of participation and apply this to schools as complex systems. Examples of 'manipulation' (Rung 1) include using community members to rubber-stamp the existing leadership agenda or implementing student surveys to cherry-pick 'desirable' results while ignoring problematic findings on other issues. For example, the earlier example of the school that hired a community hall to relocate the children perceived to be 'troublesome' during their Ofsted inspection, ensuring the inspectors only met the children deemed to reflect their values. The 'troublesome' children thus had their voices silenced. From a system perspective, manipulation limits understanding of a school's complexity by seeking to narrow the system to fit a particular view.

Table 5.2 Ladder of school participation

8.	(Citizen) control	Degrees of School Community Power
7.	Delegated power	
6.	Partnership	
5.	Placation	Degrees of Tokenism
4.	Consulting	
3.	Informing	
2.	Therapy	Non-participation
1.	Manipulation	

Arnstien (1969), *Eight Rungs on the Ladder of Citizen Participation.*

Regarding 'therapy' (Rung 2), Arnstein notes that medicalising a problem can effectively stifle participation by creating the perception that treatment is needed. For example, there is – quite rightly – a greater focus on supporting children and young people's mental health and well-being in schools. However, the conditions that threaten it – for example, bullying, exam anxiety, performance pressure, marginalisation, low staffing morale, and the like – are not part of the conversation. Thus, therapeutic participation risks overemphasising an individual's responsibility to 'cure' their *individual* problem rather than identifying and addressing the *collective* factors contributing to creating and maintaining it. Moreover, those administering the 'cure' don't necessarily reflect or acknowledge their own position and power. In failing to do so, they might be inadvertently silencing those students' voices by prescribing a pre-determined solution ('cure') rather than listening to their experiences and solutions. For example, it is often easier to focus on pay and conditions when addressing staff recruitment and retention rather than exploring staff experiences and identifying what factors attract and enhance the teaching experience. In effect, those participating in a therapeutic form cannot engage because the system perceives the problem and solution to have already been identified.

'Informing' (Rung 3) involves passing information about the proposed change to the relevant population. Arnstein expresses concern that "too frequently the emphasis is placed on a one-way flow of information – from officials to citizens – with no channel provided for feedback and no power for negotiation"[2] in this form of participation. Such one-way information flow is evident in schools that share policies with parents and students without seeking a response. Such an approach, which distributes information in one direction according to a hub-and-spoke network shape, assumes that everyone will interpret the information similarly and share the author(s)' perspective. Such participation is tokenistic, however – inaccurately equating information provision with dialogic engagement. Power is maintained via a lack of inter- and intra-group opportunities to discuss or feed back on the information presented. Suppose a leadership group decides to extend the school day for students, for example, and informs parents and students that the timetable change will happen next term via an email and a notice on the school's website. From the school leaders' perspective, they have informed the two key stakeholder groups (students and their parents) about the upcoming changes and their expected compliance. However, the consequences for both groups – and their potential concerns – have not been considered. Indeed, their perspective has not even been invited. Therefore, informing creates an asymmetric knowledge imbalance. The informer has more knowledge of the potential options than of the receiver as they have not sought genuine participation from other school stakeholders.

Arnstein considers 'consulting' (Rung 4) a more legitimate form of participation, but she is still cautionary, noting that:

> if consulting them is not combined with other modes of participation, this rung of the ladder is still a sham since it offers no assurance that

citizen concerns and ideas will be taken into account. The most frequent methods used for consulting people are attitude surveys, neighbourhood meetings, and public hearings.[3]

Unlike 'informing', 'consulting' provides a two-way communication channel. For example, administering a staff survey can provide useful information on staff needs and sub-groups. However, consultation risks being tokenistic if school staff are unclear how the school will use their response and what further action might occur (if any). Tokenistic consultation forms can seriously undermine school members' willingness to participate in the future by failing to honour the time and attention respondents invest in the process with a clear link to subsequent action/change. A second consequence is that school community members become disillusioned with consultation processes and opt out of future ones, becoming marginalised from the changes they wish to see in the school.

In addition, leaders must link stakeholder consultations to other participation forms. I was fortunate to lead a project[4] across ten primary and two secondary schools that used surveys to (*a*) understand how students perceived their ability to be kind and friendly and (*b*) ask how kind and friendly they thought their classmates were. Interestingly, students typically rated themselves as much more friendly and kind than their peers. However, while some schools did nothing with this information (tokenistic participation), others applied it fully and creatively to generate student-led marketing campaigns informing students about how kind and friendly everyone was in their school. At this end of the participation spectrum, the student consultation ultimately led to kindness workshops that generated a broader range of activities, including a flash mob in a school assembly in one case. The consultation was thus part of a wider participation strategy that *could* lead to systems change, but the range of schools' responses to the information demonstrated the various rungs of the participation ladder.

'Placation' (Rung 5) allows a select group to participate in decision-making but also carries the potential for tokenism. For example, a school might institute a representative female student group to suggest solutions for tackling sexist attitudes but only implement the minimum needed to 'satisfy' (i.e., placate) a particular group – enough to say they have acknowledged the stakeholders' opinions and concerns. Another example of placatory tokenism would be inviting a guest speaker to address sexism without taking any further action afterwards. Placation is more likely when emergent system aspect requires attention and information, raising the stakes enough that school leaders to want to be seen taking quick action but fail to recognise the broader consequences across the school.

Arnstein defines 'partnership' (Rung 6) as where "power is in fact redistributed through negotiation". Classroom agreements are a great example of this, where teachers and students jointly establish how they will interact with each other to create a positive learning environment for all. Key in this process is that all participants can express their voice and are willing to listen to others. Creating genuine partnerships requires a school's networks to recognise that other stakeholders have valid and valuable perspectives that need accommodating. Authentic partnerships enable participants to collaborate towards system change; they dissolve boundaries. However, where a working relationship is labelled as a 'partnership' but one side retains the power, participation becomes tokenistic and the disempowered group may feel exploited. Consequently, the partnership is unlikely to be stable or effective, as the label does not reflect the experience.

For example, two schools I worked with entered partnerships with the local police around the same time. In one school, the head teacher saw the police officers as an extension of his staff, telling them where to go and what to do. Consequently, few police officers wanted to work at the school. In contrast, the second school's head teacher valued the police officer's independent role, giving them a designated room for private consultations alongside access to the staffroom. As a result, students actively sought out the police officer to share their concerns and seek advice, fundamentally changing the way students and staff saw the police. As a result, the police valued the relationship with the school as a genuine partnership to protect students in the wider community.

'Delegated power' (Rung 7) gives executive decision-making capability to a group. While this form of participation enables a group to speak out and act, it is bound to a specific system feature. In the earlier example, where staff brainstormed ideas to address bullying, part of the failure was rooted in the perceived authoritative boundary. Whereas, for example, if senior leaders delegate power to staff (including budget responsibility), the group is able to successfully translate planning into action since the perceived boundaries of the means/permission have been established early on so the group has power to act. However, it can be difficult for hierarchical institutions such as schools to delegate power, as it undermines their prevailing decision-making structures (based on individual roles and authority). Delegating power also depends on a network's shape: hub-and-spoke networks may replicate existing power structures, whereas alternative network shapes can create new system behaviours in the form of participation and creativity. Delegated power places responsibilities on groups and group leaders to create opportunities for genuine exploration and creativity. However, systems leaders must integrate delegated power with networks and feedback; otherwise, they risk creating a niche in the system that limits the opportunity for wider system change.

What Arnstein calls 'Citizen control' (Rung 8) equates to community control in a school. At this point, the school community has an active role in the school's existence, as attempted in various school models in England. Under New Labour (1997–2010), the original Academy movement sought to distance school governance from Local Authorities' control to include community groups and businesses. The programme focused on converting failing schools into Academies, premised on the belief that increased community control would raise standards and address educational inequalities. Rather than specifically achieving this goal, however, the introduction of Academies created alternative models, for example, the introduction of Multi-Academy Trusts that reduced opportunities for community participation as education become corporatized.[5] In contrast, the introduction of Free Schools in 2010 enabled a range of stakeholders (including parents, teachers, charities and businesses) to set up their own schools by applying to the Department of Education. The goal of Free Schools was to increase community participation via greater freedom over the school's timings and curriculum content. Although admirable in theory, this form of participation risks already powerful community stakeholders creating a school in their own image, with other forms of tokenistic participation such as informing, consulting and/or placation featuring under the guise of offering school-community control. Yet, the ability to have full participation through the lens of schools as complex systems means that all members of the system are able to contribute to the decision and actions as well as be influenced by educational setting as a socially complex adaptive system.

5.5.2 Navigating the participation ladder

As emphasised earlier in this chapter, system leaders must understand their position in the system, the power they have and the forms of participation in their setting. Those wishing to enact change often perceive themselves as dispassionately objective agents of change, assuming they are separate from the system and that the change is for others, not for them too. We could call this latent positionality, in so much as that appearing objective is taking a position, so that either the system leader needs to be revealed by reflecting on their position or self-identified objectivity is recognized as having a position by others in the school community. Hence, it is crucial to recognise the power in positionality. A systems leader's every action interacts with the system's feedback, network shape, time experience, emergence and boundaries. I was acutely aware, during my PhD research in schools, of my own positionality and power to influence. I was repeatedly asked by staff if they were doing the right thing. On one level, this was about reassurance. On another level, however, it reflects the fact that educational advisors and consultants are often prescriptive about the changes that need to happen, so staff seek approval or want validation that their actions. In contrast, I was interested in what changes occur once educational staff begin thinking in terms of systems. Thus, I had to constantly reflect – Do *you* think you're doing the right thing? – to minimise my influence on how they wanted to change their system. I did recognise this was frustrating for them as I was not engaging with the expected rituals of performance associated with the implicit Taylorist mindset.

Adapting Arnstein's Ladder of Participation to a school context has indicated that participation in systems change is not straightforward. Instead, schools are a complex social dynamic where choices and decisions can amplify or marginalise those in the school community. People often see systems change as a linear process by which leaders collect views, generate options and implement a chosen solution.[6] However, Arnstein's Ladder of participation demonstrates how much more intricate it can be. Furthermore, the *way* systems leaders allow stakeholders to participate in the system-change process – not just the outcomes – is what fundamentally matters in terms of thinking big and thinking differently.

Returning to the primary-school example, where parents played staff against each other (see section 5.4.4), I began working with the staff to build their team dynamic and develop conflict-resolution skills. At the same time, the head teacher worked tirelessly to ensure the school had a clear vision for its relationship with the community. I then facilitated discussions with 20 parents (and a handful of staff acting as co-facilitators) about what education meant to the parents, which yielded a rich and animated conversation. Crucially, this discussion allowed parents and carers to have a *different* conversation – one focused on their perception of educational value as a community, rather than on their specific child. Recognising that there were no dads in the room, however, I ran a second session attended by three dads and two male staff that lasted 90 minutes, dominated by a discussion of the challenges of being a father and having young children. This powerful experience yielded a commitment to another session to ensure more dads attended. In both cases, we moved from isolated bounded actors to interactive staff-parent networks.

Lastly, the head teacher asked me to help the staff develop better staff-student relationships, noting the Year 3 group as being particularly volatile. Over six weeks, we ran team-building exercises and lots of circle time (where everyone sits in a circle and listens while one person speaks), and I was invited back several times to continue this work, mostly to role-model to staff. By our final session in Year 6, this group was so accustomed to circle-work that they immediately cleared their desks and sat in a circle to await the talking piece. Their teacher (who was new to the school) was awestruck at how quickly and quietly they achieved this. This vignette demonstrates how, by understanding the school's vision and how to change the relationships through weights of interaction and network shapes, a school that had been stuck in perpetual conflict became a community. As the school's community had new forms of participation and conversations, the school support increased; it received an 'outstanding' classification by Ofsted, and the head teacher won the Teacher of the Year Award. Such external acknowledgement confirmed how substantially the school had changed. For me, the real change was the playground, where you could see different exchanges in the morning and afternoon pick-up, with more smiles and laughter, the enjoyment of being a school community.

This example illustrates how participation in systems change requires a genuine desire to see perspectives from other parts of the system. Professor Checkland, who created the Soft Systems Methodology, called these 'worldviews' – mental models of the world we each build from our particular experiences, rituals and knowledge. Effective system leaders recognise that their worldview is only one of many and those who shout most loudly or passionately are nevertheless only one part of the system. Engaging with those who opt out or lack confidence that their voices will be heard is considerably more challenging, yet their views can often bring new and unique perspectives that add creativity to systems change. By engaging and collecting other people's worldviews, system leaders can deepen their understanding of the system's present state. Understanding and applying the ladder of participation helps identify how much stakeholders have been able to share their worldviews about the system and their hopes and aspirations for its future.

5.6 System language

Sensitivity to language is an essential feature of system change. Engaging with stakeholders in complex systems such as schools requires a keen awareness of how different school community members use labels and attribute meanings, which can be highly localised in the system of interest. Indeed, one can argue that language is a complex adaptive system that continuously modifies meaning to new contexts. However, for our purposes, we will explore language's importance to systems change from two perspectives: (*a*) content and (*b*) boundary construction and maintenance.

5.6.1 Language change indicates system change

Language changes often accompany system changes since a new idea, intervention or project can generate new forms of language content. For example, the term 'mental health issues' comprises a whole raft of subsidiary labels and meanings, including anxiety, resilience, mindfulness, low mood and recovery. These labels and their corresponding meanings can create potential in-groups, that is, those familiar with them and those not. Hence, we must consider whether the new language has replaced previous labels or synergised with the existing school language. For example, terms such as 'restorative' and 'trauma-informed' are often simply prefixed to existing labels, creating partial-oxymoronic-like terms such as 'restorative detention room' (a real-life example). People then assume they have achieved meaningful change because they have incorporated the new language. Instead, they have offered only a tokenistic 'nod' to the latest trend – all label and no substance. To illustrate this incongruity, we could take it to its hypothetical extreme, for example 'trauma-informed caning'. This makes the point that the new language can often dominate a system without fundamentally changing it.

Language-as-content often necessitates people to ask about its meaning, thereby revealing their lack of knowledge and potentially leaving them feeling ignorant or embarrassed. Therefore, systems leaders must be mindful of language as content, and its possible interpretation by the individuals and stakeholders with whom they seek to work. For this reason, I use group discussions to explore how different stakeholders create a shared meaning. Such discussions often reveal language adaptations such as acronyms (e.g., 'mental health' becomes 'MH') or colloquialisms (e.g., 'are you feeling rizzy [resilient] today?'), indicating a certain acceptability of use in the system. In such cases, systems leaders must monitor whether the label and its meaning stay connected. Language appropriation is a cheap form of change, but it does not mean that the *system* has changed. For example, 'mental health' might become shorthand for stress, that is, "How is your mental health today?" becomes "Are you feeling stressed today?" Cremin (2019) defines this type of language change as part of what she calls a 'masquerading system' – one that wears the 'mask' of the new language but does not embody the intended meaning or behaviour change. By recognising the importance of language in social systems, systems leaders can regulate or amplify labels and meaning through networks to promote connection. This is especially important when other school community members use their power to appropriate or reject language.

5.6.2 The language of projects and evaluations

Systems change is often accompanied by new standards-and-assessment language, which can create its own jargon. For example, the ubiquitous use of RAG ratings simplifies change into three simple colours (red, amber and green). However, I have found that terms like 'red-amber' or 'amber-green' have been introduced – and can creep into other school aspects – because the change boundaries do not neatly fit the project-management rating system. In attempting to reduce complexity, RAG ratings thus inadvertently dehumanise students, encouraging people to think about the *colour* rather than the people involved and their lived experience. Such over-simplification negates the understanding of education's primary stakeholder: the students.

The bounded use of language also includes the language of evaluation, inputs, outputs and outcomes, reflecting a perception that schools are 'complicated' rather than 'complex' systems. Evaluation quantifies the value of what already exists rather than what *could* exist, which lacks an evidence base. Evaluating complex systems requires recognising the 'who' in each evaluation component: *who* is evaluating, *who* is asking the questions, and *who* is allowed to answer? Speaking with a maths teacher on one course I supervised, we discussed his desire to use a questionnaire to explore how his students thought the school helped them engage with maths. When I asked how involved his students were in co-designing the questions and measurement scale, he was shocked to realise he had not considered their perspective on this at all, thinking of them only as respondents. This returns to my earlier point that systems leaders wanting to enact change must recognise their position and power in the system. Project-and-evaluation language can become dehumanising, creating distance between those 'implementing' and those 'receiving'. Thus, language's ability to create distance is a form of boundary creation, and school-based project management risks maintaining perceived boundaries rather than dismantling them.

5.7 Summary

This section built on the conceptual framework for understanding schools as complex adaptive systems by recognising the key aspects of social complexity, including stakeholders, language and participation. Identifying a system's stakeholders is about recognising existing networks and who belongs to them. A school community's influence is determined by the network's shape and interaction weight, which amplifies or regulates other networks and stakeholders.

Language change is a key indicator of adaptation in a system. However, depending on the system leaders' power and positionality there is the risk of language appropriation masquerading as a system change. In addition, project management and evaluation language can undermine the most human-centric opportunities for system change. While tempting, simplifying a school system's complexity only increases unexpected results.

Recognising *who* participates in systems change is central to understanding schools as systems. The participation ladder demonstrates how some rungs can create the *illusion* of participation ('manipulation' or 'therapy') without its reality. Thus, system leaders must recognise tokenistic participation forms (e.g., 'informing', 'consulting' and 'placation') that school community members may see as one-sided empty gestures, creating resentment or doubt that anything will change. System leaders must gain others' trust by enabling more authentic participation (e.g., partnerships, delegated power and community ownership) to generate system change. The best chance for enacting effective, lasting change is when school community members have a stake in the future system and can participate in its change.

Notes

1. Paulo Freire wrote extensively about the banking model of education.
2. Arnstien (1969, p. 219).
3. Arnstien (1969, p. 219).
4. This was with Professor Perkins and Professor Craig, two leading academics on social norms theory.
5. Arguably the Multi-Academy Trust becomes the Hub to the multiple schools' spokes.
6. I will have a further rant about how often I come across this in educational consultancy and want to just shout *stop!* Okay, maybe that was a little rant.

6 Systems leaders

The simplest way to introduce this chapter is to quote the American tennis player Arthur Ashe (1943–1993):

> Start where you are, use what you have, do what you can.

There is a risk in system leadership that the system's complexity can feel overwhelming, often due to outdated leadership theories specific to a particular time and ethos, which we have already covered to an extent in Chapter 2. School leadership was arguably more straightforward when education was exclusively for the wealthy or religious, when most of the population worked in fields, during the Middle Ages. Then with the rise of the industrial age, leadership focused on producing as many workers as possible to operate machinery. But as schools adapt to the needs of their communities and wider society in our post-industrial society, there is a need for school leaders to become system-aware. Leadership that still treats schools as complicated systems will be unable to recognise and thus adapt to emergent changes, with leaders seeking to maintain a system unfit for the current eco-system of its school community. In addition, leaders who seek to reduce complexity will often be surprised by unexpected changes, not because they are unaware of the change but because they are applying the wrong system model to their situation.

6.1 The myth of the hero-innovator: exposed

One of my favourite articles, entitled "The Myth of the Hero-Innovator," by Georgiades and Phillimore (1975),[1] exposes the failure of thinking that an individual can change an organisation.

This then is the myth of the hero-innovator: The idea that you can produce, by a training, a knight in shining amour, loins girded with new technology and beliefs, will assault *their* orgnisaitonal fortress and institute change both in *themselves* and other at a stroke. Such a view is ingenuous. The fact of the matter in that organizations such as schools and hosptials will, like dragons, eat hero-innovators for breakfast. (1975:315)

Importantly, they conclude a system approach in educational settings would be useful for school change. Bearing in mind they were thinking about this in the 1970s! They were way ahead of most leadership theory.

My experience of the myth of the hero-innovator was whilst working in one of the most deprived parts of South London, where five consecutive 'superheads'[2] were parachuted into one particular secondary school over three years to raise the school's low educational outcomes. However, all five 'superheads' left after failing to achieve any meaningful improvement. While undoubtedly successful in their previous schools, they and the Local Authority failed to recognise the school's fundamentally different eco-system from the ones the head teachers had developed and honed their skills in. Asking them to apply the same expertise there was akin to asking an Inuit Eskimo to build an igloo in the desert.

Thus, failure to acknowledge a school's unique eco-system often sets leaders up to fail. Furthermore, the title 'superhead' created the myth of an educational superhero who heroically and single-handedly saves a school, inclining their efforts towards individualism (trying to replicate their previous success) rather than the collectivist systems thinking necessary for understanding and improving the school. Thus, each successive superhead focused on driving and imposing change rather than recognising the system's increasing resistance to top-down management. Moreover, the rapid turnover of superheads facilitated the current system's continuation, becoming a feature of the school's culture. Eventually, one of the school's existing staff teachers became head teacher, remaining in that post for many years. By developing in and knowing the eco-system, they were able to recognise the school community's needs and dynamics from their lived experience of its history and challenges; this head teacher was able to build the school community's trust. For me, the key point is that understanding the eco-system – not just the complexity of the school but its interdependence with the community it was nested in – was vital. Alas, the superheads as hero-innovators failed to be system leaders as they did not engage with the systems which were crucial to their and the school's success.

6.2 A framework for system leadership

As developed in previous chapters, system leadership requires a framework for thinking big and differently about how school change occurs in systems. System leadership is about going beyond seductively simple hierarchical structures that presume a need for the same roles and functions regardless of time and place. Systems leaders recognise that multiple network types are necessary to initiate change and that developing new forms of feedback will help to connect different parts of the school. For example, cross-curricular themes offer a fantastic opportunity for different school aspects to connect and coordinate. In doing so, new and richer experiences are created that no single department or team could achieve on its own. Systems leadership recognises that adaptation and learning are essential for systems change. Importantly 'learning' requires failure and mistakes as the adage goes; they must 'fail fast, learn faster' to enact the change they wish to see.

This chapter explores the need for systems leaders to embrace a new mindset, avoid common cognitive traps, and develop reflective skills towards self-awareness in the system to create meaningful change.

6.3 Leadership approaches to systems

6.3.1 Intuitive system leadership

Some leaders intuitively understand systems leadership. During one INSET session in a primary Pupil Referral Unit (PRU), staff in the session challenged me by declaring they 'intuitively know their kids'. Unclear about what they were referring to, I interpreted this to mean they believed they could predict the future! However, drawing on Gary Klein's work on how professionals across multiple sectors make quick decisions (Klein, 1998), I realised they were actually describing their mental-database of pattern recognition, that is patterns in their children's behaviour and learning across different situations and time points. Using such pattern recognition, they built mental simulations of likely scenarios of when a child was in distress – a critical tool when dealing with children with significant emotional and social needs. As young children cannot necessarily articulate their requirements, they can become volatile when triggered by a perceived threat. Thus, the PRU staff needed a mental model of the child to anticipate and meet their needs *before* distress was triggered or manifested. For me, their 'intuitive' skill was spotting the early warning signs of a trigger and de-escalating the situation before the child's emotional state deteriorated so much that it disrupted learning. So, in that sense they were predicting the future! From our perspective, they were intuitively sensitive to signs of change in the complexity of their children by being attentive to small signs which provided information on the current system state that is the child, or class. I don't think any one of them would have said they have system leadership skills, but on reflecting, they clearly had an implicit framework of dealing with complex systems.

6.3.2 Decision-making and pattern recognition in systems

Similarly, systems leaders can understand intuitive aspects of their decision-making based on their position in the system and how they lead. Hence, intuitive systems thinking can be developed over time, allowing system leaders to recognise patterns and build mental simulations at speed. Most importantly, it gives leaders the confidence to act on these. Whereas, it is easy to confuse intuitive system leadership with 'experience', that is, simply having been at the school for many years but failing to understand the school as a complex adaptive system. The badge of experience, without a framework for understanding the system, runs the risk of assuming that authority on the past is sufficient for maintaining the present state of the school. However, pattern recognition develops from repeated exposure to a system-created situation, with the system leader being intentional on reflecting on the changes in them or the situation over time. For example, teachers and students become familiar with each other's typical classroom reactions and interactions as the term progresses. Eventually, the teacher can tell when something has happened to the class, and the students can tell when the teacher is having a bad day. Both have understood the regularity of the other's patterns and can recognise when something has changed.

Pattern recognition can deepen insights when system leaders are repeatedly exposed to the same dynamic, for example, the regularity of movement between classes means identifying who may have just had a really challenging lesson and needs some emotional support. In contrast, broader pattern recognition depends on exposure to a similar situation across various environments. For example, my considerable time spent discussing systems leadership with schools has deepened my understanding of school systems and the likely challenges leaders will encounter. In addition, my experience working in youth prisons and the health service has developed my understanding of systems change in different eco-systems. The key point is that the breadth of types of system helps system leaders to recognise different patterns in terms of system energy, feedback (or lack of), time, boundaries and emergence

Combining complex systems frameworks with intuitive systems leadership enables systems leaders to leverage the best analytical and intuitive elements to think big and think differently about the change they wish to see.

6.4 School management theory – the legacy of Taylorism for system leadership

Since most school management and leadership theories focus on effectiveness and efficiency, school leaders who have been taught to break systems down into their component elements may find (complex) system leadership challenging. School management and leadership emerged as recognised disciplines after comprehensive education was introduced in the UK in the 1940s, becoming common in the 1960s. Education in the UK and many other countries has become politicised since then, with political leaders discussing the need for schools to be more efficient and effective under the umbrella term 'school improvement'.

As Chapter 2 highlighted, Taylor's legacy underpins a large part of this dogma, particularly his 1911 book, *The Principles of Scientific Management*. Chapter 2 described how Taylor's ideas created a formula to maximise low-skilled workers' capacity to produce products at speed, breaking production down into a single repetitive task per person: the birth of the production line. This form of production generated reliable and replicable standardisation for a particular product. And since the production line manager had to deduce where a fault occurred – whether mechanical or human – their value lay in how efficiently they kept the production line moving and optimised the total output.

Taylor's theory evolved to become the dominant management ideology for industrial society. When applied to education, however, it presumes that schools behave like production lines that can be ever more efficient and effective in 'producing' educated young people. Thus, school improvement becomes a process with no end goal, since a school can always produce *more*. Consequently, quality-assurance processes – like the production line – focus more attention on education's *outcomes* than its *experience*. League Tables and Ofsted inspections rate a school's educational effectiveness as a *product*, not as a personal experience, embedding the idea that the 'workforce' must be monitored through data spreadsheets to track progress.

However, as outlined in Chapter 2, a post-industrial world requires a post-industrial understanding of schools' complexity. This is where systems leaders become pivotal in recognising and understanding a school's interactions and interdependencies.

6.4.1 Silo working

A compartmentalised workforce of individuals working on only one part of a system limited success to those controlling each part, leading to the rise of 'silo working'. Referring to silo containers for storing grains, 'silo working' describes a situation when different groups within the same organisation operate in separate 'containers', working independently without connection or coordination with others. 'Silo working' thus implies that a school's functions can operate with minimal or no connection to other parts of the school and is the antithesis of systems thinking, implying that an organisation's various parts can operate separately.

When applied to a school, this organisational form means individual functions do not seek to understand others or their interactions with the wider system, leading to a loss of emergence. Moreover, time is experienced linearly, as silos only measure time in relation to their own functional tasks. This may be the closest social systems like schools come to being closed networks, with minimal or no interaction within the school or its eco-system.

Silo working leads to several problems that system leaders must be aware of. Firstly, silo working often leads to territorialism, thus reduced energy sharing in the system because each silo manager focuses exclusively on maintaining their system aspect, keen to protect and optimise their particular function/team. However, in doing so, silo managers are ultimately seeking to control a complex system that does not conform to their needs or plans, creating a system dynamic where leaders feel that the only way to cope in the schools is have more control, intensifying silo working in the system.

In addition, territorialism creates communication gaps because of the limited interactive weights, meaning other parts of the system do not recognise or communicate with one another. Finally, although each silo strives to be successful, their success may come at the cost of the wider system. For example, a behavioural policy that sends misbehaving students out of class may reduce time lost due to disruptive student behaviour in the short term. Longer term, however, it may lead to a deterioration of student-staff relationships as teachers fail to get to know students and students feel disconnected from classroom community. Therefore, the policy ultimately amplifies the very thing that managers wanted to avoid, leading to more disruptive behaviour requiring more frequent ejections from the classroom. Thus, one system part's success (the behaviour policy) has come at the detriment of another system element (student-teacher relationships).

Secondly, Taylorism often dehumanises education. Uninterested in the quality or experience of work, Taylor expressed contempt for workers, suggesting that "[t]hey deliberately work as slowly as they dare while at the same time try to make those over them believe that are working fast" (1911: 33), implying they could not be trusted. If schools are treated like production lines, then any noncompliant child is thus considered 'defective', that is, failing to conform to the criteria by which the school's success is judged. Hence, educational inequality is a feature of the system, rather than a consequence. Any child which does not fit with the standardised model of education is unlikely to succeed. To paraphrase Todd Rose, rather than fitting the child to the system, we need to fit the system to the child (Rose, 2015).

Furthermore, since teaching arguably attracts those wanting to help children achieve their full potential, Taylor's legacy undermines the values and inspiration that may have motivated people to become teachers. This links to increasing staff-retention concerns, particularly of newly qualified teachers, as the growing burden of the production-line approach undermines teachers' fulfilment and joy in their professional roles – a situation the teaching profession must address.

Educationalist Sir Ken Robinson took this a step further in one of the most watched TED talks of all time, arguing that "schools kill creativity" by educating it *out* of students,[3] not because teachers lack imagination and creativity, but because the educational system prioritises efficiency and effectiveness over the learning experience. Even if school leaders manage to achieve an 'outstanding system', their only goal beyond that is to avoid any decline in outputs. Instead, system leaders must seek new opportunities to develop emergent properties that engage the school community in a new and creative future. While Taylorism may have suited the rise of mass production, standardisation and conformity in the industrial age, system leaders in a post-industrial society must embrace creative opportunities for school communities to engage with new challenges.

6.5 School leadership and types of system change

Systems leadership requires school leaders to identify the energy sources discussed in Chapter 4 (attention, information and money) to invigorate their system and address emergent challenges. To do this, system leaders can implement and influence knowledge in their schools in three main ways: partnerships, pilots and projects.

6.5.1 Partnerships – bringing new relationships into the system

Partnerships enable systems leaders to introduce new knowledge into their schools and can comprise a single partner or multiple collaborating organisations. Partnerships typically involve trust, expertise and a shared understanding of purpose. From a complexity perspective, a partnership's strength lies in the nature of the relationship, that is, its interaction weight, boundaries, experience of time and feedback forms. However, commissioning a partner in a transactional relationship may have legal compliance but does not necessarily build trust. Likewise, partners can bring high levels of trust but very little understanding into the school. I remember one deputy headteacher telling me about "a guy who is brilliant at addressing bullying who'd been bought into school". When I asked what he did, she replied that he pulled a lorry with his teeth! Although I recognised that his charisma and impressive trick had caught her attention, it was unclear what he was actually doing to equip children to address bullying.

At their worst, partnerships are a substitute for genuine educational engagement, consuming system energy but failing to contribute. When a charity asked if I would endorse their work in schools, my first question was about the potential benefits to those schools. Instead of answering, they told me about how successful the charity was in the media, how it had secured celebrity ambassadors, and that it was going to be launched in a national campaign that the schools could be involved in. This example illustrates the way partners can become parasitic, taking energy without giving anything in return – something systems leaders must be mindful of.

Conversely, partnerships demonstrating a genuine commitment to mutual benefit are the most successful. As I mentioned in the 'Loose networks' section in Chapter 3, I co-founded and ran a secondary school network in Lambeth from 2005 to 2008 that enabled members to share their practices, issues and concerns. The members' mutual acknowledgement of trust and expertise meant they often invited each other to their respective schools. Moreover, as the network expanded and the member schools began to improve, other organisations (e.g., charity, police and educational organisations) sought to collaborate with them and present their ideas and initiatives. The organisations benefited from the opportunity to access 12 proactive schools in one go, while the schools benefited from the growing collective knowledge. Mutually beneficial partnerships are the most likely to last; therefore, system leaders must quickly identify and address parasitic ones.

6.5.2 School pilots

The second type of relationship common in schools is the piloting of a new service or idea, which may be an external part of a partnership. Such pilots are often research or policy-based, led by an external organisation wishing to test its ideas in a school. In return, schools often receive brand association (e.g., with a university) or bragging rights (e.g., about being part of a government pilot that led to wider educational change). Internal school pilots often require significant investments of money and attention from system leaders, whereas external pilots typically offer formal funding via resources. For schools, pilots are often less beneficial than partnerships as they are usually time-bound and involve less change to wider systems.

Pilots are often implemented through teams that form hub-and-spoke networks, with the pilot lead as the hub. Leading a pilot is often a question of co-ordination. I was involved in a pilot across four Pupil Referral Units[4] (PRUs), where a team of experts acted as a hub for the PRU spokes. Three of the PRUs received funding, while the fourth was unfunded to test whether information and attention were sustainable without money. Each PRU had its own working group with a co-ordinator working with pupils, parents and staff. In effect, the pilot had a fractal structure (as found in chaotic systems), with self-similar hub-and-spokes replicated at different project levels. For head teachers, the pilot offered potential benefits to the school community. While the head teacher can sign off on a pilot, however, the coordinators face the challenge of building momentum for something new with staff who might feel it threatens or undermines their previous or current work, creating defensiveness on a conceptual level.

If we return to the idea of a school as a production line, then a pilot is simply a cog in the machine – it can change an aspect that helps the school to be more effective or efficient in some way, but it cannot change the production line's overall function. Thus, pilots can be an attractive way for system leaders to experiment with their school system since they do not necessitate committing to a total system change. Another fundamental issue with school pilots (one we will return to in Chapter 8) is their unsustainability in the system. There is a danger that leaders keep reaching for the next shiny idea; signing up for a pilot might *feel* like action and progress but often leaves a litany of abandoned projects that failed to achieve anything. Thus, system leaders must be cautious in engaging with pilots, which may benefit those involved in the pilot (via experience or prestige) but not necessarily the school as a complex adaptive system (as my own experiences have suggested).

6.5.3 Initiatives – the potential of emergence

Like pilots, school initiatives are often time-bound. They may also be internal or external but are often led by a single person or small team within the school. Initiatives can emerge from the school's internal networks, either in response to community issues (such as student-led activism to address climate change) or via staff wishing to develop new curriculum material. However, self-generated projects require a concerted application of system leadership skills, including amplifying desirable behaviours, transitioning bounded agents into self-organised networks via interaction weight, recognising alternative views and ensuring correct participation forms. During my PhD research, I worked with a school that brought together staff interested in addressing student behaviour with me. While the staff had assumed that this would involve a pilot, I explained that it was for *them* to decide how they wanted to change their system once they had a better understanding of system thinking, and that I had no interest in *prescribing* a pilot or bounding them in my research time frames. This was to remove the pressure of delivery in my time, whereas I wanted to track their experience of time in their system.

One suggestion they made was to organise for a behaviour specialist to talk to the students. At this point, I *did* intervene, suggesting that externalising the solution via a partnership would not lead to self-generated knowledge as they were in effect outsourcing the solution to their problem. The staff subsequently agreed to collaborate amongst themselves to develop various options for supporting staff in addressing behaviour issues with students. Some staff dropped out due to other school commitments. However, a loose network of committed staff emerged – a mix of pastoral staff, special education needs teachers, year heads and class teachers – and met to discuss options based on their shared knowledge of behaviour in the school. Their diverse perspectives enabled a broader discussion of behavioural issues, although they did not invite views from students or parents. Their project focused on equipping staff with reflective questions to ask when dealing with challenging behaviour. An aim that emerged from their perception was that staff were already competent but often rushed due to the demands of the school day, often missing opportunities to de-escalate negative behaviour or gain deeper insight into its causes. In addition, they wanted to check that their colleagues did not find the reflective tool patronising. I was impressed with the group's creativity and empathy in developing their initiative. As well as being new and innovative, their proposal met the school's specific needs and showed the potential for changing the system.

System leaders must recognise that internal creativity is more likely to be generated when the system allows the space and time for making new connections, which often means stepping outside existing school routines and rituals to explore and share; hence the importance of weight of interaction, network shapes and system energy.

6.6 System dominance

Animal hierarchies are relatively easy to spot in nature: a lion is obviously an apex predator, while gazelles are prey. In social systems such as schools, however, dominant and subservient systems are less recognisable; hence, identifying a system's power sources becomes crucial for system leaders. System behaviour can be dominant, subservient or co-dependent, and understanding which form of system behaviour is being changed and the consequences for other systems is a key aspect of system change. In a hierarchical eco-system the dominant systems themselves don't change; instead they can alter subservient systems. Conversely, while subservient systems *can* change, they cannot alter dominant systems directly. For example, the national curriculum is a dominant system, whereas the way teachers teach it is a subservient system. Moreover, multiple subservient systems may meet a dominant system's needs. For example, a school's punitive system is a dominant system made up of multiple sub-systems that maintain it: for example, detention, points,[5] restorative practice, isolation rooms,[6] or exclusion (expulsion), as chosen by a school's leaders. Irrespective of how much or little these sub-systems are used, their presence is dictated by the larger system they are part of, meaning that they are all subservient. In contrast, the dominant system can act as an attractor. Thus, even when a new intervention initially appears to be an alternative to the dominant system, it will either become subservient or co-opted over time.

For example, the organisation Trauma Informed Schools UK has become increasingly influential in helping schools support students affected by trauma or mental health problems whose behaviour has become a learning barrier. They aim to help schools "become trauma-informed and mentally healthy places for all". Trauma and mental health problems are often linked to adverse childhood experiences (ACEs[7]), which are used as indicators of health outcomes in later adult life. However, at first glance this seems to contradict a punitive system in schools, suggesting staff must be aware of behavioural triggers rooted in neuro-social responses to ACEs rather than trying to 'punish' them. There is strong evidence that trauma does affect behaviour (See van der Kolk, 2014, or Desautels, 2020). However, I will suggest that the dominant punitive system in schools will likely co-opt the trauma-informed approach. This will happen as the system: (1) only gives children deemed 'vulnerable' access to trauma-informed support, meaning its actual availability will most likely be to children that fit a stereotype of vulnerability, rather than those who are actually vulnerable; (2) schools will use trauma-informed language, but punishments will remain in place, the paradox of punishing trauma will become a form of organizational blindness (see 6.7.2) in the system; (3) a small group of committed staff will continue to champion trauma-informed approaches (until they leave); or (4) a new form of support will usurp the trauma-informed approach, yet the punitive system will remain and this new initiative will be co-opted. Point (2) echoes the points made in Section 5.6 ('System language') of the previous chapter, which highlighted how language is often used as a sticking plaster over a system's 'symptoms' without addressing the systemic cause, allowing a school to wear the 'mask' of change without embedding it. This is not to dismiss the importance of trauma-informed schools or any similar initiative, only to acknowledge how system dominance undermines a system's capacity to change in the ways we might hope.

For system leaders, recognising what is dominant and what is subservient is not as straightforward as it appears, as complex adaptive systems are dynamic by nature. Therefore, understanding dominant systems which influence the system they want to change becomes imperative. Hence, system leaders are aware of the boundaries that may need to change and how to amplify the social energy though networks to overcome, remove or subvert such boundaries. This is why system leadership requires a different lens to think big and differently if leaders are to achieve a meaningful change in their educational settings.

6.7 System leadership and cognitive traps

System leadership requires the constant ability to see the system. This is easier said than done. For example, the language of Taylorism is ever-present and needs to be guarded against.[8] To help, I have identified some of the common traps I have fallen into or seek to avoid. But this is not the definitive list by a long way, and there may be others you recognise. In terms of these cognitive traps, we will cover seeing individuals, not the system, organisational blindness and noise, how systems push back against change, and a rather controversial section on why time is never the issue for schools.

6.7.1 Seeing the individual, not the system

This cognitive trap happens when we perceive an individual to personify systems change. There is a natural tendency to see a problem and its solution as an individual one, that is, the difficult parent, the poorly behaved child or the intransigent teacher. Similarly, charismatic head teachers may attract our attention because they are good at self-promotion rather than because they are genuinely changing the school system. Leadership mythology and hierarchical structures tend to over-emphasise an individual's decisions and attributes relative to their surrounding support system, risking the perception that a single individual can change a complex adaptive system.

Equally, it is easy to blame a single individual when a system fails, particularly when they are senior. I remember working with a new head teacher known to bully his staff, although it became clear in conversation that he felt insecure about his new role and status. His staff shared this insecurity, creating the conditions for a blame culture and lack of imagination, and the students role-modelled the bullying behaviour. Thus, system members replicated the behaviour at every fractal level, with everyone too busy trying to hide the mistakenly perceived weakness of being vulnerable with each other. Though it would have been easy to blame the head teacher for these consequences, systems leaders need to ask broader questions about the head teacher's recruitment, support and the school culture he had entered. After this particular head teacher left, the new head teacher brought a team of leaders, teachers, and teaching assistants to instigate school change, profoundly affecting the school's culture and results through pro-social modelling and a nurturing ethos across the school.

Therefore, to think big and think differently, systems leaders must avoid the 'charisma' cult and focus on how the present system creates a situation where individuals are repeating the same decisions in the system of interest. By taking a systems perspective, leaders can change the situations staff members experience and the decisions they must make. In the primary school I mentioned earlier (Section 5.4.2), the new collective values and cohesion meant parents were more likely to receive the same response from all staff members, removing the possibility of playing them off against each other. By changing the interactions, we changed the context of staff-parent conversations and thus the possible decisions which could be made in the system. For this reason, systems leaders must focus on the system rather than the individual.

6.7.2 Organisational blindness

Attentional bias is another key distortion in decision-making, describing the tendency for humans to prioritise certain types of stimuli over others. This idea was made famous by the invisible gorilla-in-the-room experiment (see Chabris and Simons, 2011), which showed that people can miss unexpected but significant occurrences (such as a gorilla walking past them) when deeply focused on a task. But what happens if an entire network misses something critical because they are so focused on something else? This is what I will refer to as organisational blindness: the inability of those in the system to see a system aspect apparent to those new or external to it. If I question why a particular poster is displayed when I visit a school, for example, staff and students typically say they hadn't even noticed it – even though its whole purpose is to attract people's attention. Organisational blindness often develops because information fails to retain our attention over time; we effectively stop seeing it. However, by checking in with those who are new or aware in the school and being willing to hear their opinions, systems leaders can benefit from a fresh perspective in the system to see the system.

As already discussed in Chapter 4, organisational noise also occurs where there is so much informational overload that people become selective, prioritising the things that most matter to them (see Section 4.1, 'Attention'). There may be considerable visual 'noise' when walking down the average school corridor, for example. Similarly, focusing on a single conversation in the school playground is difficult, as the auditory noise is likely overwhelming. The ubiquitous use of emails – particularly group emails cc'ing staff – also contributes to the digital noise of managing inboxes. Hence, organizational noise leads to organizational blindness. Thus, recognizing organizational blindness can be challenging for system leaders, often because we know our system so well that familiarity and routine have obscured our clarity and ability to challenge the familiar.

Therefore, when considering changing a school system, systems leaders must first recognise how effective communication is within the school community. A system leader must navigate the organisational noise to amplify the change they wish to see.

Lastly, organisational noise can relate to the legacy of old projects, pilots or partnerships because there is no motivation to remove information that is no longer relevant. Systems leaders must ensure space for new information to grow, which may mean removing old or outdated information. Systems leaders can easily fall into the trap of generating more organisational noise or blindness unless they are mindful of the forms of communication they use and the fact that a system's energy is finite.

6.7.3 Systems pushback

While any change in a complex system will cause a reaction, many leaders fail to expect this. I believe this is because they perceive the system as a complicated one, seeing it as stable and predictable. However, socially complex systems such as schools have learnt to adapt to their present system state, allowing them to survive or thrive in the wider eco-system. System boundaries help 'contain' the system, protecting it from being so adaptive that its instability brings it to the point of exhaustion.

6.7.3.1 Explicit resistance

There is a common perception of the 'old guard' – a group of teachers who refuse to come onboard with a new change or initiative and whose voices are the loudest resistance to change. Nevertheless, this system defence is useful, as it will clarify the aspects they reject and those they seek to maintain. For example, dynamic tension might arise from leaders wanting to amplify a new system aspect such as newer software, for example, staff who are keen to use new software versus those who want to continue using the current software. These two forms of feedback create a system pushback. Depending on which group has greater access to system energy, one will become dominant and the other subservient.

When thinking about school system change, I often draw on Rogers' Diffusion of Innovations theory (1962), which explains how, why, and how fast an idea or innovation spreads through a population or social system. I suggest that diffusion works similarly to amplification. Figure 6.1 is based on Rogers' diagram called: Adopter Categorization on the Basis of Innovativeness, which outlines Rogers' explanation of how different stakeholders respond to innovation. Rogers divides adopters into five categories: innovators (2.5%), early adopters (13.5%), early majority (34%), late majority (34%) and laggards (16%). If we apply these to schools, innovators are willing to take a risk on a new initiative, stake their reputation on it, and learn from failures. Early adopters quickly see the benefits of the innovators' work to the school's practice and community, swiftly following suit. The early majority take longer, waiting until an innovation shows demonstrable benefits beyond the innovators'/early adopters' enthusiasm before adopting it themselves. In effect, they wait for evidence of success. The late majority are more sceptical, waiting to

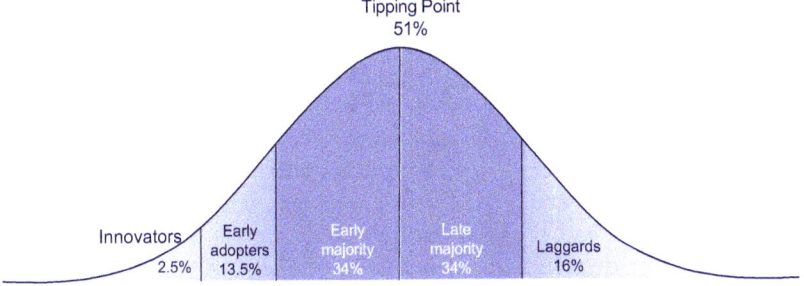

Figure 6.1 Adopter Categorization in Rogers' Diffusion of Innovation Theory.

see whether the innovation spreads sufficiently through the school to become part of school policy. Finally, laggards either resist the innovation completely or are the last to adopt it, as it threatens their familiar ways.

For system leaders, the critical point about system pushback is the considerable time spent convincing laggards (16%) to embrace change. However, given that system leaders need 51% onboard with an innovation for a social system to reach a tipping point, I would argue that their focus is better directed towards building networks to embrace innovators, early adopters and the early majority. System leaders must find the path of least resistance to avoid system pushback. The key then becomes how to move the late majority by 1% to tip the system into a new way of behaving. Systems leaders need to recognise system pushback as a natural response to change in schools rather than seeing it as something to be overcome, understanding that it indicates system aspects that some members seek to maintain. In flowing and guiding rather than opposing and resisting, addressing system pushback thus resembles Tai Chi, a Chinese martial art based on keeping one's balance while finding moments where the opponent overcommits and loses balance. Similarly, system leaders must find ways to nudge the balance of the system to tip into a new way of being.

6.7.3.2 Implicit resistance: the act of omission

The second form of system pushback is when the system agrees with the change but does nothing to enact it, like the power to opt-out in network, which is less obvious than direct opposition. Oppositional system feedback manifests via amplified behaviours or regulatory responses, clearly identifying perceived boundaries (e.g., a lack of time or money) and real boundaries (e.g., space and people's ability to attend) that system leaders can acknowledge and address. In contrast, passive system pushback is identifiable only by the *absence* of action, that is, inaction as a form of action (or no feedback as feedback). The skill of the systems leader lies in recognising and addressing acts of omission – arguably the most challenging aspect of system leadership, but one that management thinking rarely acknowledges. The late organisational theorist Russell Ackoff noted in a BBC Radio interview (2009) that we are much more likely to blame people for things they *did* (but shouldn't have) than things they *didn't* do (but should have). The act of omission in schools can be justified in many ways, the most common being "We didn't have time to do this". As we explored in Chapter 3, since time is relative to other parts of the system in complex adaptive systems, it is always available in schools. It took me a long time to realise that, rather than there not being *time* in social systems to do something, there isn't enough *social energy* – that is attention, information and money. Therefore, acts of omission often reflect a school's inability or lack of desire to focus enough of its finite attention on a particular issue.

6.8 Time in schools is never the issue

Often there is the cry in school that "we don't have time". However, for system leaders time is never the issue because depending on what type of system they are engaged with, they will understand how time is perceived. In complex adaptive systems, we have already suggested that time is relative to other things happening in the system. In this way time in a dominant system will always override the needs of subservient systems. An example is a staff focus group I ran in one school to discuss systems change. Since the session took place at the end of the school day, I checked in with staff as they arrived to see how their day had been. It became evident that some were still in the past, reflecting on events that had happened that day, while others were already in the future, considering the next task requiring their attention once the focus group finished. For me, this indicated that other – dominant – systems occupied more of their social energy than my lowly subservient research project. I concluded that this passive form of system pushback was not due to the staff's lack of intention or goodwill but other system aspects demanding their attention. For me, this insight was revelatory, explaining why systems change fails to happen even when people genuinely want it.

Instead of giving in to frustration at the slow speed of change, systems leaders must thus identify which dominant system is diverting energy from the subservient system that could enable change. The absence of action is itself feedback, indicating energy not time is the issue in the school system.

6.9 Summary

The four cognitive traps highlighted in this section are not an exhaustive list. Rather, I have shared them to help systems leaders recognise – and avoid – the major pitfalls. Of these, solving problems by focusing on the individuals involved rather than the system they operate in is the biggest, possibly because leadership and head teacher mythology tend to idolise the lone champion able to enact systemic change. However, the reality of schools' complexity means that teams and networks – not individuals – are fundamental to successful system change.

System leaders must also recognise organisational noise and blindness, which requires awareness of their position in the system and how they communicate to other parts.

System leaders must also recognise and embrace system pushback, which is often omitted from discussions about school change, and understand that school community members do not 'receive' the prospect of change uniformly. Instead, some may be innovators wanting immediate change while others may be laggards, refusing to shift no matter the evidence or the school community's needs. Thus, the context of change is as important as its content.

Finally, system leaders must recognise that 'nothing happening' is a sign that the school system cannot spare enough energy to enact the system change. Analysing dominant and subservient systems will help identify the cause(s), so system leaders should not give up. Instead, I hope this chapter has highlighted the opportunity to recognise this form of system behaviour as passive system pushback, enabling system leaders to find new and creative ways to engage the present system. The next chapter explores how to implement system change.

Notes

1. The term "hero-innovator" is often used but it I rarely referenced back to Georgiades and Phillimore.
2. Specialist head teachers with a track record of outstanding success were appointed to quickly reorganise and refocus schools perceived to be failing.
3. "Do Schools Kill Creativity?" (June 2006); "Bring on the Learning Revolution!" (May 2010); "How to Escape Education's Death Valley".
4. London Councils – Back on Track: Evaluation of Restorative Approaches.
5. Points accumulate over a day and then the student earns a punishment, for example, a student is sent to the isolation room.
6. I use this label to correspond with the experience. However, schools often use alternative terms such as 'inclusion room', 'internal exclusion' or 'exclusion room'.
7. Examples of ACEs are alcoholic parents, domestic violence and child abuse, to name but a few.
8. This has been a challenge in writing this book where it would be so easy to put 'input' or 'outcome', for example.

7 Leading system change

This chapter explores how system leaders can implement changes that create authentic transformation in their school's system. Drawing on the conceptual frameworks developed in previous chapters, we begin applying these ideas to initiating systems change. Our conceptual framework provides a complex adaptive model enabling system leaders to think on a different scale and level. We will be exploring how system leaders move from theory to application. This chapter returns to stakeholder engagement, worldviews, mental models, sources of system in the social system, as well as revealing our system of interest through system mapping, system artefacts and creating possible future systems. Thus, this chapter demonstrates the considerable breadth and quantity of interrelated areas involved in applying system leadership to be able to think big and differently.

7.1 Is the school community ready? (and who cares?)

Just because system leaders immersed in their system sense the need for change does not mean different stakeholder are ready, let alone willing, to change. Exploring the need for system change may be straightforward: change in the cohort of students, challenges in retaining staff, shifting parent and carer perceptions of the school. Recognising the readiness may entail willingness to form new networks, shift boundaries or focus attention. This raises a conundrum: wait too long to prepare the system to be ready and you miss the opportunity; go to soon and expect the system to push back if not resist the change altogether. Hence, the importance of understanding networks, positionality and power with engaging with stakeholders; it will help to identify who else cares. This is different from having the responsibility for change. In understanding who else cares, system leaders can create new network shapes, through weight of interaction, to amplify support for the emergent change. In doing so, their network helps to make ready the system for the change to come.

7.2 What do we mean by system change?

A school's systems change typically takes one of three primary forms: survive, thrive or decline. The first, survive, depends on identifying requirements for the system's survival, which necessitates engagement with stakeholders to ascertain the nature and extent of the school's needs. For this reason, it is crucial that system leaders understand stakeholder participation. The second, thrive, identifies opportunities for the school to thrive by creating new and emergent system features. The third, decline, is when the system loses its ability to maintain features of complexity such as social energy, the creativity of emergence, and the feedback senses to engage interdependently with other systems in its eco-system. All three can types can involve either incremental or radical change, depending on what is happening both within the system and across boundaries in the eco-system.

System *metamorphosis* is where the system transforms entirely from one form of being to another, and breaks the link with past and present states of being. Distinct from radical change, where the system still retains existing features, metamorphosis involves changes in the interdependencies and interconnections that create an entirely new set of capabilities and behaviours to survive or thrive.

7.3 Initial stakeholder engagement: school history matters

System leaders engaging with stakeholders early in a systems-change initiative must recognise that stakeholders hold valuable aspects of the system's collective 'memory'. Component-based change experts often want to offer pre-existing solutions, disregarding the unique background insights different stakeholders can provide and their indication of the system's readiness or resistance to change based on its history. A school's history is often evident in various forms, including its reputation, achievements and the shared narrative of its organisational culture, physical layout, displayed posters, policies and student work. For example, I was once in newly built school which had a beautifully pristine interior.[1] After 18 months, there were still no displays of student work, hence no representation of the student population. Rather than simply displaying corporate posters featuring smiling students, I suggested showcasing students' work demonstrates and celebrates an authentic presence. It is in the creation of a system artifacts where different stakeholders contribute, which represents a tangible aspect of the school community. The young history of the school, after 18 months, meant it had lacked participation and had demonstrated an absence of student engagement. Conversely, some private schools I have worked in are steeped in history, they have artefacts giving an instant sense of the rituals and traditions binding the community together.

By engaging with stakeholders, system leaders gain insight into the long-standing traditions which indicate dominating systems as well as more recent events at the forefront of community members' minds; this helps system leaders to understand the narrative[2] in different stakeholder networks. I remember working in one school following a pupil's death due to a knife crime. When I spoke to the pupils, they expressed anger that the staff had not done more to prevent this young man's death. At the same time, the staff grieved the loss of their pupil but felt unsupported by senior leadership, while senior leadership felt abandoned by local authority services. The common theme emerging after this recent tragic and traumatic event was the expectation that the school would continue to run as normal. However, without any space for grief, compassion or reassurance, relationships deteriorated. Traumatic events are disproportionately memorable and thus more likely to become part of the school's history than everyday successes. Thus, system leaders must tune into a school's historical narrative when considering the system's change they wish to bring about, identifying whether to engage or overhaul the historical narrative.

A school's history matters because it provides system leaders with a map of how the school system arrived at its present state. The next task is to determine how far this is a shared historical narrative or whether different stakeholders relate different perceptions of the school's history. For example, do female students have a different experience of school lifts compared to male students, for example, sexism and sexual harassment? Or do different departments have different narratives about underfunding versus over-resourcing? Identifying deviations from the dominant school narrative identifies potential sources of conflict or unmet needs the system leader may need to address.

Finally, the school's prevailing leadership narrative provides valuable information. When I returned to my old secondary school as a Local Authority Consultant at the time, I remember speaking to the same dinner ladies who worked there when I was a pupil. Although they did not remember me (I had never attended lunches), I was struck by their relationships with students and parents and their views on head teachers. Since their collective memory spanned over 40 years in the school, they could compare head teachers in a way few others could, providing a unique and valuable perspective on how well the current school leadership was managing its system. Yet, they were not recognised as invaluable living history because of their low status in the hierarchy of the school.

From a systems perspective, the most valuable information in a school's history lies not in its facts but in its insights into how the school narrative binds shared views across various stakeholder groups. Therefore, system leaders must be mindful of their personal worldview when engaging with others' historical narratives, which may bias them when stakeholders share alternative accounts or even worse, unwittingly discourage them from sharing their unique experiences – particularly among marginalised groups. History matters in socially complex systems; it tells how the educational setting got to be the way it is in its own unique way.

7.4 Initial mental models

A school's history matters because it sheds light on its stakeholders' narratives and perceptions. As part of a socially complex system, these stories connect and interact to generate new, emergent features. Therefore, systems leaders must seek to recognise the 'range of truths' within a school rather than pursuing a single 'truth'. To this end, I have found it useful to explore how stakeholders define the change they seek to implement – whether that be inclusive pedagogy, mental health or cyberbullying. It is crucial for system leaders to identify and recognize how different community members perceive the school. Such initial mental models are more fluid than community members perceive, however, no matter how confidently they may project their initial position.

As we have already seen, language matters (Chapter 3, "Boundaries", and Chapter 4, "Information as energy") and is part of history, helping us understand whether there is a shared meaning within and across stakeholder groups. Asking stakeholders to define key terms demonstrates their initial mental models and the extent of language amplification or regulation happening across stakeholder groups. For example, the consistency of language, such as terminology, may hide the lack of accuracy across stakeholder groups. For example, ask staff, What does discipline mean? For will instantly accesss their initial mental models, but as we shall language can help shift such positions to richer and more insight mental models.

7.5 Language as a way to understand mental models

Differences in definitions also indicate boundaries between stakeholder groups, as educational language has its own jargon, creating in-groups and out-groups. A highly valued shared jargon indicates an in-group whose common lingo may have little meaning or relevance for those outside the group. This is relevant if a system leader seeks to implement a change in a context lacking previous awareness of or exposure to the new intervention or initiative. In such instances, stakeholders' interpretations of the new proposal can be revealing and informative. The system leader must then decide how much background information to provide when investigating the nature of stakeholders' 'interpretive lens'. 'Digital neglect' offers a good example: while school staff may combine their existing definition of 'digital' with the safeguarding-training definition of 'neglect', thus assembling their own definition for understanding the issue, students may generate a range of different meanings based on their unique experiences of the digital environment and what they consider as adult 'neglect'. The system leader can then analyse commonalities and differences within and between groups to develop a potential system definition of 'digital neglect'.

In addition, it is crucial to recognise the emotional context of the story being told when exploring stakeholders' narratives. Returning to the school tragedy mentioned earlier, it was clear that students felt considerable anger towards the staff alongside their sadness and grief over the loss. However, I saw no evidence of school staff or senior leadership engaging with students' experiences or sharing their perspectives of the event. With no shared space for dialogue, emotional expression and understanding, student and staff relationships thus deteriorated. This is not uncommon for schools affected by a traumatic event, where relationships can deteriorate because mental models of the event are not shared or acknowledged. School leaders are often anxious to return to the 'production line' model of a complicated system as quickly as possible, failing to recognise the profound consequences of a school's emotional climate when traumatic events occur. However, by understanding the system's emotional context, leaders can recognise how different stakeholders will engage with the change they seek.

Overlaying a system's emotional context with Rogers' innovation diffusion, innovators are likely to be excited about change, seeing how it meets a particular system need. Early adopters may be slightly more cautious, wanting to see evidence of benefit. In contrast, the 'early majority'[3] must align the change with their existing beliefs, for example, improving school inclusivity by providing more diverse reading material aligns with my belief in the value of all members of the school community. The late majority tends to be more sceptical, seeking evidence of success to reassure them that the change is of value and worthwhile participating in. Lastly, laggards are typically change-averse, either responding with aggression and anger (emotionally demanding for them and system leaders) or pessimistically dismissive that the change will make any real difference. Recognising and meeting the emotional needs of innovators, early adopters and the early majority means keeping them involved and informed about the proposed change, bolstering their receptivity and enthusiasm for it. Addressing the late majority is a lesser priority at this stage, as it takes time to build an evidence base demonstrating the proposed change's success. Engaging with laggards is often an emotionally draining exercise in futility and unlikely to tip the school system into a new behavioural pattern. So, system leaders need to be astute with where they want the flow of social energy to go.

In addition, it is vital that system leaders recognise their own emotional efficacy in this context: how they model optimism and enthusiasm can inspire and attract others towards the change they wish to see. It is important to know and understand systems, theories and solutions, but system leaders also require emotional self-awareness, realising that confidence is contagious and can be amplified in schools. If the system leader radiates confidence in the proposed change, the school community is more likely to follow their lead. Equally, if staff believe that the school community is changing and they are part of the change, pupils are more likely to feel the same. However, the same is true in the opposite direction: if staff firmly believe that change is unachievable and the school will deteriorate regardless, their fatalism will be equally contagious. As confidence has a network effect, systems leaders need to identify school-community members who are resolutely confident about the benefits (and, therefore, potential influencers) and whether their certainty presumes success or failure.

A health warning: charisma is not the same as confidence. Rather, system leaders' confidence comes from logically applying the concepts and framework to the appropriate participation activities to understand the system's needs.

7.6 Ways to visualise your educational settings as a system

This section will introduce a range of techniques that have been used to map systems. The decision on which technique to use (or all of them) will be in your hands, depending on the depth you want to explore your system in.

7.6.1 Mental maps

As a systems leader, you will start developing your own mental map of your school's system through initial engagement with stakeholders. Figure 7.1, shows a basic mental map. For illustrative purposes, I have used an example based on vulnerable students (available in Microsoft Word's SmartArt).

By identifying the different stakeholder categories in a single year group, this map helps explore how each stakeholder group defines and understands the meaning of 'vulnerable' and classifies particular students as 'vulnerable'. These findings can then be discussed with teachers and teaching assistants to establish whether they share the same understanding of what 'vulnerable' means and to whom it applies. Finally, this vulnerable/non-vulnerable classification could be extended to older students in the school to assess whether vulnerability changes with age. Likewise, exploring younger students' understanding may reveal limitations or incompleteness in their definitions, increasing their vulnerability to risks not yet part of their understanding of vulnerability. Thus, the mental map enables systems leaders to develop questions highlighting the presence or absence of interconnections within the system they seek to change. But ... mental maps are static; they do not show the dynamics of the system, but rather help to see what is within the system.

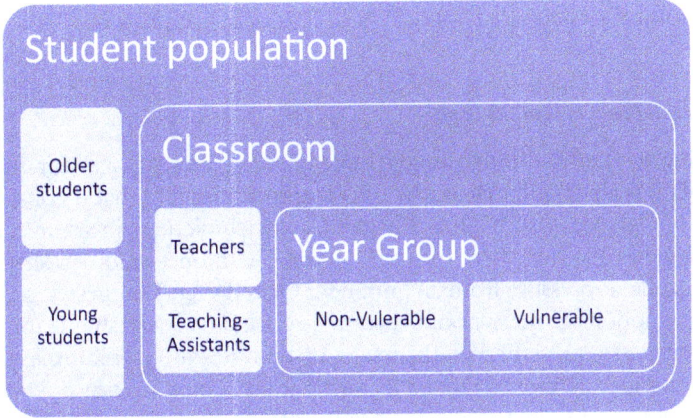

Figure 7.1 System mapping vulnerable students in school.

7.6.2 Rich pictures

A Rich Picture is a way of identifying, exploring and defining a situation and expressing it in imagery, providing a preliminary mental model for discussion and dialogue towards a shared understanding. Peter Checkland and Jim Scholes' work (1999) on Soft Systems Methodology (SSM) utilised rich pictures as a useful way to see how stakeholders build their mental maps, and importantly, start to put in aspects which capture the dynamics in the system. Rich pictures use a range of pictures, for example, a person who might represent students, a symbol for school finance, and text, explaining how poverty impacts student resources. The key point is to capture the relationships in the rich picture. However, when I tried to apply SSM's rich-picture process to schools, I found it needed adapting – in part because I think it was developed in an engineering context, presuming some knowledge of mapping engineering processes. So, I found it useful to be explicit about capturing the relationship rather than staff being overly concerned with how well the rich picture looked. While the SSM process is undoubtedly useful in some sectors, I found that rich pictures worked best in schools when combined with metaphors (see below).

When working with schools I have found analysing rich pictures helped staff and students to understand feedback in the system, and sources of energy, creating a shared understanding of how the school system looks for those within it. As such, rich pictures are a powerful means to facilitate a collective understanding of a school system's present state. Moreover, a co-constructed rich picture provides a collaborative process for stakeholders to share perspectives and find commonality. While comments about artistic quality or representativeness are common, these aspects are unimportant for systems leaders; what matters most is what the imagery represents for those creating it, this means process is more important than what the group produces. The rich picture may become a system artefact; in one school the senior leadership team added their rich pictures as evidence during an inspection on how they would be changing the school, having used a collaborative approach.

7.6.3 Developing a school metaphor

According to the Cambridge English Dictionary, a metaphor is "an expression that describes a person or object by referring to something that is considered to possess similar qualities".[4] When I began using rich pictures in schools, staff often struggled to know where to start. Working with one senior leadership team under particular pressure from an imminent Ofsted visit, I suggested coming up with a metaphor for the school's current system. The leadership team decided that it was best represented by the image of a jungle with a volcano in the middle. The jungle represented that a lot of what was going on was difficult to see and that now and then a major explosion from particularly vulnerable students resulted in a massive fallout for the school. I then invited the staff to draw their metaphor, suggesting they consider factors that amplify the volcano's energy and those that help contain a full eruption during volcanic moments in the school, providing a way for staff to identify amplification and regulation within their system. What was interesting was how quickly there was agreement about the metaphor and how they all had experiences of being in the jungle and being present during a volcanic explosion. They were using the metaphor to create shared language of their experiences in the system.

The choice of metaphor should be left to those in the system, as I would suggest they are best placed to describe and articulate the school's system and culture. I remember one occasion where staff described their school as a very 'safe' place, choosing a barred window to represent this sense of security. The chosen metaphor was particularly interesting because the school had recorded the highest number of exclusions in the area the previous year and was known for its Draconian discipline policy. Their metaphor clearly linked safety and imprisonment. It was particularly illuminating from a systems perspective, on how there was a shared agreement on this, but also on how challenging it would be to change it. Moreover, the window's bars indicated that the system was perceived as immovably rigid and fixed to keep students and staff safe. I think the "safe" was staff acknowledging students were from a very deprived community, whereas this metaphor did not acknowledge the great work the school did outreaching and support families in very challenging situations.

Metaphors thus offer systems leaders deeper insights into the intuitive ways stakeholders perceive their system. For example, while working with a Multi-Academy Trust, I asked head teachers in the room to provide metaphors symbolising what the Trust meant to them. One group compared themselves to a Star Wars rebellion seeking to change the Empire (an educational system that devalues staff, students and communities). Another group likened themselves to D'Artagnan and the Three Musketeers, quoting "one for all and all for one" to describe their sense of being in it together. I noted their metaphor's underlying theme of fighting oppression, just as D'Artagnan and the Three Musketeers fought against Cardinal Richelieu. Although the head teacher's sense of social justice had been implicit, using metaphors to visualise the system made it explicit. Therefore, system leaders can use metaphor as a springboard for helping their school community to visualise its system through a metaphor. Doing so with stakeholder groups helps explain the common recurrent features across discussions, such as system members' needs where disconnects are amplified through the school. For me, I have used the metaphors of the machine and nature to juxtaposition the difference in managerial thinking versus engaging with complex systems. See figure 7.2, to help visualise the difference and what this means for leaders in being able to think big and differently.

7.6.4 Visualisation matters

Before we move on, one of the things I said is that "systems are hidden in the everyday". Using some or all of these techniques helps the school community

Figure 7.2 Metaphor of machine and nature systems.

to see they system. But … it is never truly accurate. The more stakeholders engage, the more useful it is to see both where there is shared understanding and how a dynamic is using energy in the system. All visualisations are a representation of reality and, importantly, can be changed. If a metaphor is not working, change it or combine it. The point for system leaders is to see how visualisation helps them and others to think differently, rather than writing a school action plan or reviewing policies in a ritualised way. Please don't feel restricted to the techniques suggested. If there are others you find more useful, then do apply them!

7.7 Creating a present system statement: what the school is doing now

Drawing on the Soft System Methodology (SSM) created by Checkland and Scholes (1999), use the process of creating a "root definition" statement: ask three questions to generate a statement.[5] I adapted the SSM process in my research, as I found responses were more forthcoming by educators when I asked those interested in changing the system in schools to answer the following questions:

1. What is the system (we are interested in) doing at the moment?
2. Whom does it currently benefit?
3. How does it do this?

The answers to these three questions help formulate the school's 'present system statement'. This process can generate considerable discussion among stakeholders, especially about who benefits from the current system, while the final question identifies the behaviours underpinning the current system.

By creating a present system statement, system leaders can support school community members through metaphor and rich pictures to help transform an implicit understanding of the school's interactions into an explicit, co-constructed visualization. As such, system statements help identify, describe and define social systems, enabling system leaders to better understand what their system is doing at the present from different perspectives.

Since developing systems statements are a group activity, there is a risk that members set aside their personal beliefs to achieve consensus and please the group leader (or one another). To mitigate such 'groupthink', system leaders must test the system statement's resonance with peers, stakeholders or external partners. This validation exercise also increases school members' involvement and participation as well as providing validation.

At other points it may become apparent to those participating in a system statement that the present system is not benefiting any members of the school community. At these points, it is important to validate that this is not a about people or personalities but rather that this is the system state, because it may have not been revealed in this way before. This is why the second aspect is moving from the present to possible future states on the system.

7.8 A vision for the school in the future

Our one-dimensional perception of time is moving from the present to the future, which is bound in a Newtonian clockwork-universe metaphor and mechanised via a measuring instrument that excludes history. System leaders face the challenge of understanding how difficult it can be for staff to be in the present when thinking about tasks that relate to decisions made in the past. There may be the temptation to blame or reminisce in nostalgia about the 'good old days'. Educational leaders often make plans for ubiquitous action, compiling lists of actions they believe will improve the school. However, action plans only tell you at best what it is you are doing now to change various components of the *system*. I emphasise the word 'system' here: if you consider the quantity of action plans schools often have, how much time might it take for those actions to combine to create a system change?

Moreover, there is a difference between envisaging *a result* and envisaging a *future system*. Where schools seek simply to survive, for example, by improving their Ofsted rating, leaders can envisage a new result, plan it and then enact the plan. However, results-oriented thinking leads to a stop-start process for systems change: progress happens because a certain outcome is required at a specific time, which stokes the system's energy. Once the result is achieved, the system's energy dwindles; hence, the issue re-emerges and a new action plan is needed. This is why systems leaders must be mindful not to prioritise the system's results and outcomes (terms I tend to avoid) over its long-term trajectory and continuity of the system.

Envisaging a future system requires creativity and imagination. Therefore, it is important to remove perceived constraints when facilitating such discussions, that is, if money was no object or there was maximum staff recruitment. It is critical at this point to ensure that those envisaging the future are not drawn into present or historical concerns. Envisaging the future requires imagining alternative paths the system could take, often underpinned by a school's values and vision of how it wants to be in its eco-system. These provide a springboard for discussing their relevance for future systems. For example, the school may envision improving community learning through increased inclusivity, respect and diversity. However, given external community changes such as gentrification, increasing private accommodation and greater family mobility (loss of intergenerational attendance at the school), it is important to consider how this future community will interpret its vision and values. Exploring possible future scenarios in a group or team allows participants to share their knowledge. In these exercises, I have found that people naturally tend to picture the worst-case scenarios; therefore, leaders must facilitate more optimistic possibilities to encourage more inspiring and constructive future outcomes. The three main trajectories are thus: survive, thrive or decline.

Involving stakeholders by inviting them to envisage the school's future can be a powerful way of uncovering trends and insights. Systems leaders can then utilise these insights to build future scenarios. For example, my PhD research addressed parent and student concerns that cyberbullying needed to be dealt with in the school – not because of existing problems, but because they recognised it as a rapidly evolving issue highly responsive to trends among children and young people. However, the school staff group who gathered to discuss the school's future system completely neglected this issue, even when I flagged it as a consistent trend across stakeholder interviews and mental models. Since the staff were clearly informed, this act of omission indicated they were unwilling to engage with the issue of cyberbullying as part of the system change. From my perspective, this was a lost opportunity to meaningfully interact with parents and students about a matter of concern to them.

7.8.1 Visualizing the future of our school

In the same way we have explored the present, many of the techniques can be used to visualise the future. Importantly, the pressure on school means members of the school may have short time horizons based on financial year, academic year, student journey, which is five to seven years. I tend to go for a much longer time horizon. For example, what will this school be doing 30 years from now? This takes those participating outside of the rituals and thinking of normal time horizons to be more imaginative.[6]

7.8.2 Future school metaphors

Metaphors of a school offer a valuable tool for members to envisage its possible future system. Future metaphors allow those seeking systemic change to envisage a new eco-system for the school – not just a new school system – and help envisage new interconnections and interdependencies.

One school I worked in chose a boat being battered in an ocean of external conditions as their school metaphor. In this metaphor, the outer conditions represented competition with other schools, Ofsted and uncertainty about the future. However, when the leadership team began envisaging a future system, their discussions coalesced on the idea of the school as a coral reef. This metaphor focused on providing increased shelter for the school's diversity and greater stability for its overall eco-system, allowing leaders and staff to understand the school and its wider community better. It was impressive to see how envisaging a metaphor for the school's future system that was aligned with their values and vision shifted their present system's metaphor. As such, I typically allow groups to test a metaphor of 'destruction', enabling them to dismantle the characteristics their school needs until the metaphor no longer works. Allowing participants to change and blend metaphors is a powerful part of the creative process when freed from the constraints of the present.

The key to envisaging future metaphors is approaching them playfully without being overly prescriptive. When facilitating these discussions, I am mindful not to offer my own suggestions when inviting stakeholders to build their metaphors, avoiding any risk that they fixate on my externally derived metaphor or conclude that there is an appropriate or inappropriate way to describe their school's future. For this reason, systems leaders must be mindful of their own positionality, recognising that they can inadvertently recruit participants into their personal vision of what the school should be, rather than gaining the range of options on what it could be.

It can be interesting for different stakeholder groups to share their versions of the future system using these metaphors, precipitating a discussion about which metaphor(s) work best individually and together. Different groups' discussions can provide systems leaders with clues to possible areas of consensus about what school's future could look, feel and be like. Allowing stakeholders to contribute to creating the future is one of the best ways to involve them in the school community.

7.8.3 From the future to the present: future system statement

Just as an architect designs a structure before building it, metaphors are a way of designing the future before living it. However, schools often do the opposite: enact change without recognising the downstream effects on the school's future system. In contrast, building and visualising a school's future system allows system leaders to work backwards from the future to the present, mapping out the trajectory to identify what needs to happen. We can use the same questions again with a slight modification:

1. What is the system (we are interested in) doing in the future?
2. Whom does it benefit then?
3. How does it do this?

It may be useful to compare the present system statement with the future one to see if there are differences. Even a single word in a system statement can prove a mental block to acceptance. For example, I remember checking a system statement with young people who disliked using the word 'creativity' in the context of "[enabling] the community to creatively solve problems in the school". One young person who did not view herself as a creative person (about which other group members disagreed with her) felt this put too much pressure on students to come up with innovative, out-of-the-box solutions. After inviting them to suggest alternatives, the sentence was reworded into "[enabling] the school community to respectfully solve problems in the school". Following this tweak in the wording, the young people happily agreed with the system statement without concern.

At other points, the present system statement may be exactly what everyone agrees the system should be doing, and therefore the present system statement also represents the future system statement adequately.

7.9 Leading system change

A key point is that system leaders cannot directly implement a new school state in the present; the school community can change only the *system*, ultimately leading to a new future state. Within this, systems leaders must recognise their existing networks and the role of feedback in creating emergent properties of that future system state. Importantly, system leaders must resist the temptation to implement a hub-and-spoke network, if other network shapes can provide greater participation in developing the future system. A system leader asks how this network can amplify and regulate the change they seek and identify which of the present system's real and perceived boundaries need shifting, altering or removing to enable that future system.

To understand a complex adaptive system's features, school leaders can use systems' energy to tip the present system into new organisational trajectories. Information about what the system will need in the future can be communicated across different networks. Engaging stakeholders who have been included in envisaging the future can be a powerful way to convey further information through their networks. However, stakeholders who have been excluded from this process are likely to be resistant to system change. System leaders engaging with marginalised stakeholders will help to avoid system pushback as well as groups feeling the changes are designed to benefit those in charge rather than benefit them. In addition, it is crucial for system leaders to capture and manage stakeholders' attention, as the present can always impede upon the envisaged future. Hence, the future system state must be relevant and relatable to the school community so that stakeholders can clearly see the need being met. The skills of the system leaders are vital in ensuring that the future system statement relates to all aspects of the school community, as this will require new flows in system energy.

A warning: There is a temptation to create an action plan that inevitably arises amid all the hard work of envisaging a future system state. This has been one of the biggest pitfalls, as school leaders put so much into understanding their system only to end with the ubiquitous action plan. Therefore, systems leaders in complex adaptive systems must understand change differently than in complicated systems. While I will explore this further in the sustainability chapter, for now, we will look at some potential system artefacts that need to be created and implemented to achieve systemic change and the importance of ensuring that systems leaders retain the appropriate motivation.

7.10 System artefacts

The challenge for system leaders initiating change is to identify the system artefacts they need to create, that is, objects, experiences or places imbued with meaning that can enable action and memory for the school community. To this end, systems artefacts can be created in collaboration with different stakeholders to enhance their relevance and relatability, strengthening their meaning. Even where it is assumed that a particular stakeholder will embrace system artefacts, there is no guarantee of acceptance. Therefore, system leaders must be cautious about distributing information via simple cut-and-paste methods, as these often show either a lack of knowledge or lack of engagement. School policies are a great example of system artefacts when they are treated as a component, and show more about lack of engagement in the system than what the policy is designed to do. These are likely to be rejected as tokenistic participation forms that suggest the system leader is trying to implement change on the cheap, increasing the likelihood of stakeholder rejection.

By creating meaningful system artefacts to act as reminders for the social system they belong to is an important aspect of systems change. This is often achieved through in-service training, with staff taking notes or being given a handout of PowerPoint slides. While both have the potential to be systems artefacts, as well as school actions plans, they are usually discarded for the rest of the school year. While a range of things can become system artefacts, system leaders must intentionally design artefacts to maximise interaction with the change they wish to implement. For example, informative materials such as policy documents, workbooks, flowcharts, posters, training manuals or computer software are all ways of creating system artefacts. However, they do not necessarily engage stakeholders. System artefacts must successfully hold stakeholders' attention as well as provide information, reinforcing systems change and providing tangible evidence of systems change for the system leaders and school community. For example, using isolation rooms in schools creates a range of artefacts that reinforce the sense of isolation, whether it be desks facing the wall or signs reminding students to be silent. These system artefacts gain attention and become symbols of meaning for the school community. Similarly, posters, stress balls and bean bags in therapeutic school rooms demonstrate a range of systems artefacts, and thus are different symbols of meaning. The decision as to which system artefacts gain funding shows the dominance of one system over the other in the school community.

For change to be effective, system leaders must also remove artefacts inhibiting their systems change. This requires an awareness of organisational blindness and noise: the system artefacts school staff no longer see or interact with still use space. Whereas artefacts which still require attention from the old system create competing distractions in which new system artefacts can quickly be lost. System leaders must be mindful of addressing organisational blindness and noise when creating and placing systems artefacts in the school community.

7.11 Space and place in schools

Schools do not always consider *where* artefacts are shared, assuming everyone receives the same information. A great example I find in schools are the notice boards, which get the highest attention. However, places and spaces have a history, and places can have multiple spaces. It is important to ascertain how the different stakeholders engaging with systems change perceive space and place. Do students and parents perceive the space to be neutral, or do they associate it with emotions such as embarrassment or anger? What are the last memories staff associate with the space and place staff training is due to take place? As mentioned earlier, I was told I had done well to keep staff seated during one particular training I ran, which tells me that the training ritual for that specific school was one of boredom and frustration rather than learning and insight. Another experience I had was in several primary schools I worked in. I was told the teaching staff would be a particularly tough crowd because the last trainer had been inadequate on their subject knowledge and patronising to the staff. The defensiveness was not personal but likely to be directed at whoever was next person to train in that space after such a poor training experience.[7] The ritual's place and space created an organisational memory that needed overcoming to share new knowledge to instigate system change. Hence, systems leaders must recognise when to challenge the school's existing space and places and when to maintain them.

Systems artefacts must be positioned in the space and place to maximise their potential. In schools, I find it helpful to consider where the prime attention 'real estate' is when looking to enact systems change. For example, where are people most likely to pay attention: while queueing outside the dining hall or coming into class? And to what extent might anything already occupying the space be replaceable? Something dated represents an opportunity to replace it with something new. Also, removing other informational noise (of other posters or policy notices, for example) reduces the risk of the new artefact becoming lost in the visual information overload common in schools.

By recognising and understanding the importance of a school's spaces and places, systems leaders can help colleagues, students and parents share their views and perceptions of the system. Furthermore, they can utilise spaces and places to create new experiences and generate systems artefacts that support the systems change they wish to see in their school community.

7.12 Implementing a goal-oriented system

For a system leader, it is tempting when first presented with a report or assessment to succumb to avoidance-driven action, wanting to reduce that problem in the school: for example, less exclusions, less racism, less homophobia, less time spent out of class, or fewer hours lost to low-level disruptive behaviour. However, while leaders often want *less* of an aspect of the system, the degree to which they wish to *remove* the problem is unclear. For example, do they want to reduce homophobia by 5%, 10%, 50%, 99% or 100% or staff absence by 10%, 25% or 75%? The fundamental point is that their focus remains on the problem they seek to avoid, inevitably leading to an action plan to reduce it. The production-line metaphor thus returns; in avoidance-orientated problem-solving, the problems hinder the efficiency and effectiveness of the school as a complicated system.

My concern about avoidance-orientated motivation is the tendency for schools to focus on what they *don't* want rather than what they *do* want. I was once in a café where a customer was placing an order with the waitress said, "I don't want eggs, I don't want beans, I don't want toast", to which the waitress replied, "Well, what do you want me to tell the chef to cook?" This perfectly illustrates the benefits of switching to a goal-oriented approach in system change. Assuming a system can give *less* of something misses the key point: the system already has a 'present' behavioural pattern; therefore, the *system* needs a goal(s) to generate a new 'future' pattern.

The future system statement and vision offer invaluable tools for achieving this, helping systems leaders recognise and define what the school community needs to achieve together. Developing a goal-oriented approach to system change prevents system leaders from wasting system energy on reducing integral features of the system (often consequences of the overall system's nature) and focusing efforts on developing new patterns and behaviour. For example, a harsh behavioural policy that sent non-compliant students out of class meant teachers lost many relationship skills necessary for student management and escalation. While the leadership team sought to reduce the number of students sent out of class, it failed to recognise that the school's present system perpetuated this outcome rather than analysing an individual teacher's motives or their class's behaviour. Hence, the critical question for a system leader is what new system can they create that fosters teachers' confidence in discussing behavioural issues with students without students perceiving it as tokenism. Instead of trying to change the consequences (avoidance-oriented motivation[8]), system leaders must seek to change the systems (goal-oriented motivation). Defining and articulating goals enables them to think outside the box and develop creative system innovations that generate a new and improved social eco-system.

7.13 Resistance to change in schools

Implementing school change from a systems perspective engages with complexity rather than seeking to reduce it; resistance to change is often seen as something to be overcome with the old mantra "they either need to get on board or get off". However, we have already identified that the system will push back, and system leaders will need to be ready for this. This pushback is not always malicious; hence, the more we engage in participatory processes, the less likely the system will encounter pushback that is unexpected. The techniques for leading system change are powerful not because they use a special or mystical form of change, but because I would suggest they enable voices to be heard, the co-construction of meaning and language, and shared mental models.

There is also a second aspect, which is the resistance to change in the system leader. The more you find out about the system, the more your own position may need to adapt to understand the present system and its resistance. Finding new ways to connect and share can be seen as something others have to do. The ability of the system leader to display these skills and transmit them through their networks is where they are mostly likely to find emergence or at least create the conditions for this, which will bring about change in the school community.

7.14 Summary

This chapter has sought to provide a bridge between the concepts we have covered in previous chapters, and techniques to all system leaders to apply in their settings. The power of visualising systems is in capturing the dynamics of the past and present and what this means for the present system state. The underlying principle has been that co-construction of meaning though the visualisation techniques will enable system leaders to get a sense of what the system is doing at present. This leads to the decision on what needs to thrive, what can survive and what needs to die.

Then there is the question of what a future system state could be. This is a different perspective from setting and organisational vision where we start in the present and aim for the future. Rather, the future system statement starts in the future; and what the system would be doing then. The system leaders and networks then work backwards to understand what they did to get there. By doing this they can play with the trajectories that could happen to get them there. School and educational settings have traditionally had very stable eco-systems in regard to the communities they are nested within. Now, the wider change in society and on the planet means that leaders are going to be thinking more about future system states as information comes in and they have to adapt. This leads to our final chapter on how to sustain the change beyond the momentum of implementation.

Notes

1 For some reason this always reminded me of the Starship *Enterprise* in *Star Trek*.
2 The narrative is the story people tell, that is, their narration, about themselves and other members of the school community.

3 Returning to Rogers' diffusion of innovation types.
4 System leaders would do well to distinguish between a metaphor and a simile. A metaphor utilises common similarities with something else, e.g., my comparison of education to a production line draws on the commonalities of components, a forward march of time and mechanical production. In contrast, a simile likens a school to a production line, e.g., the school is a busy production line today.
5 (P = do) How do we do it? (Q = because) why do we do it?, and (R = result) to achieve?
6 Playing with time, I find it is surprising how many educators think that AI and robots will replace them in the next 30 years, so it is important to balance pessimistic futures with optimistic ones.
7 I did manage to create an engaging space though lots of validation of their opinions, as well as get my points across!
8 We could suggest that in a Taylorist world, the machine is always working perfectly so the only thing to do is avoid malfunction.

8 Sustaining systems change in educational settings

The previous chapter explored what system leaders need to implement systems change. Building on that foundation, this chapter helps system leaders cognitively shift from implementation to sustainability by understanding what systems change requires to survive and thrive in a school. But what do we mean by 'sustainability'? Numerous definitions exist. For example, the Cambridge Dictionary defines sustainability as continuing over a time period. In contrast, *The Limits of Growth* – the monumental 1972 work that was a springboard for the environmental movement – did not define sustainability directly but as a state of economic and environmental equilibrium:

> The state of global equilibrium could be designed so that the basic material needs of each person on earth are satisfied and each person has an equal opportunity to realise his individual human potential.
> (1972, p. 24)

This interpretation infers sustainability from a stable equilibrium between society and its environment. The concept of sustainability is closely associated with the environmental movement but is also used in leadership theory and, increasingly, educational leadership. Hence, Hargreaves and Fink – key thinkers in educational leadership – define sustainability as follows:

> Sustainability is concerned with developing and preserving what matters, spreads, and lasts in ways that create positive connections and development among people and do no harm to others in the present or in the future.
> (2006, p. 17)

This definition has important implications for schools, where systems leaders must ensure that the current use of system energy is not at the expense of future student/staff generations. Numerous other definitions exist, but their overarching focus is still on connecting the present and the future in a way that benefits humans. Educational sustainability is thus about preserving a school community's values. However, sustainability cannot be achieved through action plans, whose inherent use of targets returns leaders to a mechanistic way

DOI: 10.4324/9781003179108-8

of thinking that counters sustainable change. Instead, the ability to envisage futures – through system maps, system statements and school metaphors – will help system leaders sustain what matters most. Therefore, systems leaders must recognise that they need a different set of skills to sustain a school community's values. However, definitions of sustainability can be misleadingly simplistic, suggesting that achieving balance in a system automatically benefits its members. However, it is just as possible to sustain a dysfunctional system as a healthy and one that encourages growth. Moreover, such definitions often imply the whole system can be preserved sustainably, whereas preservation is often about negotiating between the present and the future.

This chapter identifies some key factors system leaders must be aware of to successfully navigate this complexity and explores the major challenges to sustainability in schools and what culture means through the lens of collective memory. Among these is the human predisposition towards the 'nostalgia' trap, whereby our rose-tinted view of the past inclines us to resist or reject the present and future. Systems leaders must therefore be aware of path dependency in complex adaptive systems, which causes harm, and the importance of developing sustainable systems in achieving their future system state.

8.1 Models of sustainability (or not?)

Let us now turn to what models of sustainability are presently used in educational settings. We will return to the myth of the hero-innovator, as well as explore pockets of practice, the most common model being the whole school approach, as well as schools nested in an eco-system. When thinking about school change, I saw, early in my career, schools as complicated systems, I worked with over 300 schools across London during my time in Local Authorities' educational departments, writing policies, delivering training, role-modelling behaviour and celebrating occasional successes. I diligently followed national guidance on implementing change effectively, gave school talks, engaged with partner organisations and even presented at ministerial events. But then I began witnessing the long-term life-cycle of the systems changes I'd helped initiate as they started to unravel and decay. I was at a point of frustration, I had done everything that was required from a national perspective, followed best practices. Then I was invited to give a keynote speech at a restorative practice conference in 2010. I thus shared these frustrations during a keynote at a conference entitled "Why Restorative Approaches Fail in Schools". My keynote intended to stimulate a discussion on my growing concern on the lack of sustainability; instead, it was met with muted clapping and a ferocious Q&A session. Why? Because I did not present what the audience wanted or expected to hear. At a time when the educational community was fully geared towards implementation, I'd begun seeing the enervation of restorative practice which was leading to decay – these observations were not what an audience seeking to learn how to implement had come to hear. Though offering new insights to help achieve sustainable change in schools, I was thus labelled a heretic. As described in the introduction, however, this ultimately led to the

114 *Sustaining systems change*

conversation with Professor Hilary Cremin that gave rise to my PhD. She wisely said, "You need evidence to back up your claim".[1]

This section summarises that work, presenting my reflections and findings on types of school change and a more refined critique of their sustainability. I have organised these according to the four main types of school change (Figure 8.1):

Figure 8.1 Types of school change: are they sustainable?

'the myth of hero-innovators', 'pockets of practice', the 'whole-school' approach, and the 'school as a complex system within a larger eco-system'.

8.1.1 The myth of the hero-innovator

According to Georgiades and Phillimore (1975), underlying the myth of the hero-innovator is the premise that a single individual can change an organisation – which may well have been true at some point in history, for example, for a village school whose teacher is also the headmaster. In such cases, the individual's ability to change the organisational culture was often based on the school community's recognition of their expertise and the relative homogeneity between the school and the community, since it is easier to promote an idea among people who look, act and think the same. However, Georgiades and Phillimore explain why this idea is destined to fail within the complexity of schools, drawing firstly on Katz and Khan's work (1966), which stated that:

> The essential weakness of the individual approach to organisational change is the psychological fallacy of concentrating upon individuals without regard to the role of relationships that constitute the social systems in which they are part. The assumption is being made that since organisations are made up of individuals, we can change the organisation by changing those individuals. This is not so much an illogical proposition as it is an oversimplification which neglects the interrelationships of people in an organisational structure and fails to point to aspects of individual behaviour which need to be changed.
> (Katz and Kahn 1966, in Georgiades and Phillimore 1975, p. 314)

In short, the belief that individuals can sustain organisational change in complex systems such as schools focuses on the actor rather than the system they are acting in. Moreover, assuming that a single member of staff can generate a collective transformation mistakes the system for its components. As discussed throughout this book, systems leaders must focus on a system's actions and interdependencies. With this insight, Georgiades and Phillimore articulated the myth of the hero-innovator:

> The idea that you can produce, by training, a knight in shining armour who, loins girded with new technology and beliefs, will assault his organisational fortress and institute changes both in himself and others at a stroke...
> (Georgiades and Phillimore 1975, p. 315)

In this instance, "you" refers to school leaders who believe that by sending staff members on external training courses, they can expect them to change the school for the better simply by virtue of their newly acquired information. However, as Georgiades and Phillimore argue, "such a view is ingenuous.

The fact of the matter is that organisations such as schools, like dragons, eat hero-innovators for breakfast" (Georgiades and Phillimore 1975, p. 315). Hence, the sustainability of change deriving from a single actor is a myth. Still, the leadership movement likes to perpetuate the myth of the hero-innovator' the suggestion that head teachers or inspirational experts can fundamentally change a system they enter is the first part of a fallacy. Furthermore, the second part of the fallacy is the deeper consequence of the myth of the hero-innovator, which is that such change fails to be sustainable, as it is personality-dependent. As a consequence, this form of school change is never sustainable because the individual embodies the change, and not the system.

During my master's research in Education, I spoke with a deputy head teacher who was clearly passionate about her project. She had been in the school for more than ten years. However, my analysis[2] revealed the fragility of her project's hub-and-spoke network, since there was little amplification in the system when an individual embodied a change because other parts of the network lacked the requisite weight of interaction. Due to the network shape, knowledge was centralised in the hub, and the spokes no longer had sufficient system energy to interact once the hub went. In addition, hubs always fail to connect spokes with each other, hence the shape of this network. At best, after the hub, in the form of individual (but it could also be a team), if they leave, they may become bounded actors;[3] at worst, knowledge becomes individualised. Thus, an embodied hero-innovator has an expiry date – when they leave the school, the change they effected will decline and, ultimately, disappear. As my analysis predicted, this project lost its champion (hub) when the deputy head teacher left the school a year later and collapsed when other staff members (spokes) began leaving. The passion and enthusiasm with which staff believed in the project was lost as the system features declined and the culture of the school changed, leading to the school closing.

On a broader scale, the school network I created in a local authority collapsed because I was the hub. Although I had tried to ensure a shared space and congenial relationships, the ability to coordinate the network through system energy (attention and information) meant the network lost a form of amplification, and schools stopped connecting with no weight of interaction. Therefore, the network collapsed and, frustratingly, the schools thus lost their collectively accumulated knowledge.

8.1.2 *Pockets of practice*

Skinns et al. (2009) used the term 'pockets of practice' for a type of change where a school does not commit to wider change until the experimental 'pocket' shows success. I would suggest that 'pockets of practice' could run the risk of being another term for pilots. However, if we think of a 'pocket of practice' as a niche in the system, we can broaden our understanding of how subsystems and micro-cultures can survive in the broader school system. A pocket of practice is smaller than the system it is nested in, sharing many aspects of the larger system but at a much smaller scale. However, while a pocket of practice lacks the power to impose itself on more dominant features of the school system, it can defend its place and space and potentially opt out of wider system aspects. Nevertheless, it must draw on some form of system energy to survive.

A pocket of practice may regulate system amplification. For example, I worked with two fantastic teaching assistants (TAs) who specialised in dealing with vulnerable and challenging children. Receiving numerous referrals from across the school and managing a very high workload, their work was unlike anything else offered in the school and was supported by the head teacher and staff. Their value to the wider school system allowed them to continue as a 'pocket of practice'. However, the leadership did not give them the support or resources to expand, limiting their leverage for influencing the broader school culture. The 'pocket' would collapse if they left, rendering them hero-innovators. Alternatively, the school could replace them, changing the personnel but retaining the pocket of practice.

While a pocket is unlikely to acquire more resources once established (and thus cannot amplify), it can regulate itself to survive. In this case, the TAs were given a room no bigger than a broom cupboard to work in; this consequentially limited and 'contained' their pocket of practice. The second key aspect of a pocket of practice is its boundaries. Boundaries between the dominant system and the pocket of practice are maintained by restricting the resources and energy that would enable it to grow and amplify. Alternatively, a pocket of practice can be bounded by those already within it; a sense of in-group identity, narrative and experience can make it difficult for perceived outsiders to breach it. Part of this is an experience in the pocket of practice that differs from the dominant system. Systems leaders must be aware that experiences and judgements particular to a pocket of practice may amplify its micro-culture. Returning to the example of the two TAs, the highly inclusive, caring culture they created to support students contrasted with the school's more general performance-driven approach. Therefore, students' experiences within the pocket of practice differed from those in the dominant school system.

A pocket of practice can also become a toxic space in a school. For example, unresolved staffroom conflict can lead to an unpleasantly divisive pocket of practice, with staff either avoiding the staff room entirely, exiting it as quickly as possible or perpetuating the tensions. A toxic staffroom thus has a detrimental effect on staff motivation and relationships. For systems leaders, recognising a pocket of practice that creates dysfunctional micro-behaviours (such as a disharmonious staffroom) means being aware of the dominant system's ability to tolerate it and identifying the energy sources it relies on to survive.

Pockets of practice can also survive for long periods within schools. This can be either as part of a range of sustainable pockets co-existing in the school or where there is conflict with other pockets of practice. The dominant system may allow a whole range of pockets of practice to survive within it (e.g., restorative practice, trauma-informed practice or mindfulness), for example, but they must compete with each other to retain funding, creating system fragility and insecurity. Systems leaders must be careful not to mistake a pocket of practice as evidence of systems change.[4] While it can exemplify good practice or showcase success, it is not indicative of broader system change. Indeed, a pocket of practice may inhibit systems leaders' ability to think big and think differently by rendering them organisationally blind or contributing to yet more organisational noise. Moreover, multiple pockets of practice – particularly those in conflict – can negatively affect the broader system as competition, and conflict drains system energy hindering the ability of the overall system to thrive.

There is an argument to be made that silo working – where a sub-set of the system pursues its own particular goal in relative isolation from the larger system[5] – equates to a pocket of practice. However, I would argue that a silo actively seeks to maintain its boundaries in the system, whereas a pocket of practice has the potential to amplify itself if the boundaries are removed. Moreover, silo working precludes collaboration, leading to communication gaps in the system that mean high-performing silos may exist in a failing school. Suppose we imagine the school system as a network of train tracks. In that case, silo working means that individual groups may be laying high-quality, well-engineered sections of tracks, yet fail to connect with other groups' sections – thus the train cannot run.

A pocket of practice may either be of no benefit to a school system (i.e., commensalism), mutually beneficial for the pocket of practice *and* the system, or parasitic. The parasitic pocket of practice takes social energy from the system to the detriment of the wider system, this could be in various forms: attention, in the form of the charismatic speaker; information in the form of lots of requests for data on a project; or money in terms of both staff time and actual costs for a initiative led by a charismatic speaker.[6] The system leader's skill lies in ascertaining which is most likely for the pocket of practice and whether it will benefit the school in achieving a future system state.

8.1.3 The whole-school approach

The whole-school approach is a widely used implementation model focused on the entire school rather than pockets of practice, individuals or groups. Therefore, it is broadly advocated as the model of school change by government and researchers as well as charities and educational change consultants as the recommended approach for leaders wanting to improve schools.[7] For me as a professional in education, having championed the whole-school model of change, I applied it unquestionably when I began working with schools in my early career. However – and this is a *big* however – what evidence is there for the success of the whole-school approach?

I began asking myself this question when the schools I'd worked with started losing momentum in their systems change – even though they had changed their policies, trained their staff, demonstrated success, conducted before-and-after evaluations and secured their senior leadership's buy-in. Nonetheless, they failed to show *sustainable* change. Why? Ultimately, the whole-school approach is a prescriptive one. While it gives leaders a means to implement change by writing policy, training staff and consulting students, it is too broad and mechanistic to tackle the underlying complexities of schools and prevents leaders from thinking creatively. Its limitations lie not in its content but in its non-specific, blanket generality. What is meant by 'whole', for example? Does it mean 100% of the school community or 100% of the teaching staff? The assumption is that there is an understanding of 'whole' as equivalent to 'all'. Rogers' diffusion-of-innovation model makes it clear leaders will never get 100% of stakeholders to buy into their proposed change. Thus, 'whole' can only ever refer to 'most of' or the 'majority'. As mentioned in Chapters 5 and 7, language *matters* – yet school leaders rarely question what 'whole' means in this context.

Similarly, the 'school approach' has become an evolving task list for school leaders. Thus, while the whole-school approach originally represented a simple system (i.e., write a school policy, train staff members accordingly and evaluate the results), it has since expanded into a list of tasks schools must complete. Such tasks include consulting students and parents, developing a robust Red, Amber, Green–rated action plan, undertaking before-and-after evaluations, setting up a working group and organising INSET training. The whole-school approach thus reflects a complicated system that approximates the production-line method, implicitly assuming that a school can continuously improve. Moreover, the ubiquity of the whole-school approach means very few school leaders challenge this idea. Let us do so now.

I suggest that the whole-school approach is like icing on a cake; whatever you choose to cover it with doesn't change the cake's underlying structure. Hence, the whole-school approach provides only a 'veneer' of change without fundamentally altering the school system. Suppose a school wants to claim itself to be more action-orientated regarding climate change, for example, but this could any topic. In seeking to address climate change, it might consult with students, write an action policy and accompanying plan, train staff on climate awareness, put posters up in the corridors and organise a 'green action' week for students to encourage their parents to recycle. Indeed, they may have even won an award for their efforts in promoting environmental sustainability and be asked to support other schools. Does this example represent a whole-school approach? I'd suggest not, because the whole-school approach (the 'icing') has not fundamentally changed the school's dominant structure (the cake), in this case as a source of pollution which contributes to climate change. In our example school, paper continues to be wasted on printed school resources, and the inefficient boiler remains, lights and computers are left on after school and over the holidays. Furthermore, the costs of transitioning to green energy are prohibitive for the school, requiring fundamental infrastructure changes. Hence, regardless of the example chosen, the critical point is that the whole-school approach is a cosmetic change rather than a system change, like applying concealer to unhealthy skin. It is a seductive approach because it gives the *impression* of a broader shift in system behaviour. Though this approach is widespread in education, systems leaders must therefore be wary of the whole-school approach, for which the evidence for success remains low in terms of implementation, let alone sustainability.

The challenge to the whole-school approach also comes in its application. Although research and policy often advocate the whole-school approach, a closer look at the evidence from the research on restorative practice shows while often advocated in recommendations and guidance, in a review of the research literature, only one in four schools managed to successfully implement a whole-school approach to bullying and restorative practice within 18 months to two years (Youth Justice Board,[8] 2005; Skinns et al., 2009; Wong et al., 2010; Roberts, 2013; Roberts, 2020; Bonell et al., 2018). From the evidence, this suggests a low success rate for a widely advocated model of change in the educational system change. Furthermore, findings from this literature indicated that schools tended to do one of two things at the end of this period, which was between 18 months to three years: (*a*) take the best aspect of what the learn over the whole school approach, and incorporate them into dominant systems, hence the language remains but the concept and behaviors fade, or (*b*) revert to its pre-existing behaviour (equivalent to the icing falling off the cake). While it can be tempting to continuously 'refresh' the icing, this only changes the outer veneer, not the dominant system's fundamental features. Thus, I hope to have illustrated why the whole-school approach does not offer a sustainable form of school change. At best, it is a prescriptive method for implementing change; at worst, it is a tokenistic form of change, which leaves school leaders with uncertainty on what to do after the implementation phase. Therefore, when considering the sustainability of school change, systems leaders must challenge advocates of the whole-school approach, as this model may engender change fatigue. The whole-school approach can consume a considerable amount of the school's system energy. However, since a system's energy is finite, 'constant improvement' management approaches will fatigue it if it cannot recharge or find new energy sources to sustain it.

While the whole-school approach appears to offer a shiny new solution to a systemic problem, systems leaders must recognise that by prescribing externally conceived change rather than facilitating its emergence from *within* the school, it fails to understand schools as complex adaptive systems. This may explain why so few schools ultimately sustain this form of change, as the school community's localised needs change and adapt the whole school approach fails to keep up.

8.1.4 A school is a complex system within a larger eco-system

Our final model of school change is about understanding a school as a complex adaptive system. This awakens systems leaders to the interdependencies and interconnections of school change. Schools are nested within larger communities (I deliberately use the plural 'communities' here, as schools rarely have high levels of self-similarity with their community). Increasing diversity within communities means schools must adapt to a range of constantly evolving needs (and I use 'diversity' in its broadest sense, i.e., cultures, lived experiences and worldviews rather than individual characteristics). A school community's diversity enables system leaders to engage with new perspectives and worldviews, which can help address challenges in the systems. Unfortunately, strategies such as the whole-school approach tend to negate diversity through prescriptive change, marginalising the school and local community's needs. Where system leaders face a lack of diversity, they must seek alternative perspectives to ensure that such homogeneity does not lead to organisational blindness by assuming everyone is the same.

Another crucial aspect of a school's eco-system is the wider community's stability. Schools nested within highly stable local communities benefit from the constancy of the relationship between the school and its community. However, this stability can also lead to an equilibrium that yields little need – and thus opportunity – for creativity. For example, I was working with a school in an affluent part of London. The school had good examination results and delivered these on a yearly basis. Yet, in my conversations with students and parents, there was a growing concern regarding social media and online harms. However, the school decided to take no action, as this would disrupt the equilibrium which existed with the school community.[9] In contrast, other schools face significant local change or disruption. For example, a Manchester-based school I worked with that was once part of one of the most deprived areas in the city now finds itself surrounded by enormous residential tower blocks. Since more young families rent flats, this major housing change stimulated a demographic shift, dividing the community into older residents (who had lived there a long time and were connected to the area and its history) and younger, newly arrived residents. As the leadership were aware of the greater disconnect in the community, the school intentionally became a space to bring the new and old communities together. Just as system leaders must be aware of their positionality within a school, they must also be mindful of the interplay between the school and the local community, that is, the local eco-system. Leaders who imagine their school sits in splendid isolation from the local community will inevitably be surprised when neighbourhood changes affect the school. Moreover, a local community's stability can be seductive, creating a familiarity whereby school leaders seek only to maintain the status quo rather than find new ways for the system to thrive.

In viewing a school as a Complex Adaptive System, systems leaders can draw on the complexity framework outlined in Chapter 3, which consists of:

- **Feedback**: amplification and regulation
- **Self-organisation**: the weight of interactions and network shapes
- **Emergence**: guided and organic
- **Boundaries**: perceived and real
- **Time**: relative to the features of the system and its eco-system.

This framework thus allows system leaders not just to understand their system's dynamics and their relevance to sustaining the change they wish to see. For example, while the amplification of student numbers may seem a success, it is limited by the school's physical boundaries. Similarly, amplifying ways to increase staff wellbeing will be limited by pressures (regulatory forces) by meeting agendas and performance indicators. Thus, leaders must understand the limits of change to recognise its sustainability. Moreover, it is crucial to understand the energy needs necessary to sustain change, which is why pilots often fail; the time required by the systems means there is rarely enough time for a change to embed (become interconnected and interdependent) in the school's eco-system. In addition, the legacy of production-line thinking means the primary focus is typically on generating outcomes – the equivalent of expecting a flower to bloom on demand.

Therefore, schools rarely consider how much energy pilots require to become established as a niche or systemic change in the school. If they did, they would recognise that the energy necessary for implementing systemic change differs from the energy needed to sustain it. While schools often pour most of their resources into implementing change, far more energy[10] is required to fully embed it within the eco-system – that is, to synergise it with other systems (dominant or subservient).

To maintain a complex system such as a school, system leaders must recognise what needs space and nurture to grow, what needs curating and what needs discarding. A system leader is thus a system conductor; they must understand where system energy needs to go to enable systemic change and direct it accordingly. To do so may require them to address system conflicts and find solutions that facilitate change. One common system conflict lies in sourcing the energy to amplify: finding the time and space to distribute information while retaining staff/student attention is always challenging. Therefore, system leaders must identify mutually beneficial approaches that maximise opportunity in the system for members of the school community.

As system conductors, system leaders must seek ongoing opportunities to share and discuss systemic changes with their networks. The traditional once-a-year INSET ritual is a fallacy: assuming staff can retain and apply all information delivered in a hall or gym fails to recognise that memory itself is a complex process. I remember working with one school's senior leadership team, for example. Having discussed the importance of their school values in the first session, they remarked two weeks later when I returned that "none of us can remember the conversation; we just remember we had a good time, so that is why we're back". They explained what a hectic two weeks they'd had, including an Ofsted inspection. This information told me they needed a safe space to decompress and that my sessions with them were like a bubble, a fragile moment in time to connect and be reflective. System leaders seeking to embed change must appreciate that change needs curating in a way that helps retain the school community's attention. For this reason, engagement with system artefacts becomes essential. They are touchstones encouraging members to remember and enthuse the school's values and vision as the school's system evolves.

Just as pruning stimulates new growth in plants, system leaders must begin discarding old features once they have embedded and curated change in their system. While this may be uncomfortable – especially for leaders identifying as 'nurturers' – schools have a finite amount of energy. Dominant systems either absorb subservient systems or offer no feedback in the fight for survival, thus ending the change. Therefore, system leaders must be alert for parasitic features and remove them as quickly as possible, as such features deplete system energy without equal returns to the school community. For example, I once saw a school pay vast amounts of money to an educational consultant, not because he changed their system but because of the kudos of working with him. While great for his reputation, this achieved nothing for the school community.

Secondly, system leaders need to identify and remove aspects of change that create organisational noise and are no longer relevant. This process is equivalent to weeding: removing that which is unwanted or unnecessary. The amount of outdated or irrelevant information in schools is extraordinary. I remember walking around a school that had implemented a well-being programme years before. Although the school no longer used it, the programme's remains still littered the corridors with paper-mâché models and posters, adding to the school's organisational noise. Without processes to discard what no longer matters to the system, such redundant artefacts accumulate, occupying space and attention that might otherwise support the school's current vision and goals. Removing such organisational noise can free up attention and communication channels. Therefore, to sustain change, system leaders and their networks must shift their focus to embedding, curating and discarding, which allows their school's complex adaptive system to survive and then thrive.

8.2 Systems of harm

It is vital that systems leaders identify and engage with a system's ability to sustain a particular behaviour. Systems leaders rarely have a blank sheet to design a new system. Instead, they must address existing systems to bring about system change. Prevailing systems – particularly dominant ones – have a powerfully attractive force, especially those that cause harm. The educational sector continues to discuss staff workload and retention concerns, offering new ideas to increase their well-being, salaries and status. Such ideas often address one system aspect but fail to fundamentally change its overarching patterns of behavior; new staff teachers quickly feel overworked and abandon the profession, further disillusioning students and senior staff. Thus, a narrative often emerges that the new generation of educationalists doesn't have what it takes. However, I would argue this interpretation fails to see how the system has changed the educationalist's role. Systems of harm embed tolerance, allowing harmful behaviour to continue and normalise.

In turn, normalisation leads to organisational blindness; those immersed in the system no longer see that they are helping perpetuate the very things they would consider outrageous in another context. There was a complaint in one school I worked with that students were always late getting ready for class and settling down. However, it was clear from navigating the school's four storeys and long corridors that student lateness and readiness to learn depended on two other aspects: the distance students had to travel between classes and their teachers' transition times. Firstly, the school timetable made no allowance for student's transition time from one lesson to another. Short of teleportation, there was no physical way students could arrive promptly for back-to-back lessons. Secondly, the schedule did not allow the teaching staff any transition time. Thus, even when students were waiting at the classroom door, the teaching staff might not have made their way there yet.

In this example, tardy students or staff are easy to blame, but they were not the real issue. Instead, the problem stemmed from a dominant system of planning and the failure to recognise it. No one connected the commute between classrooms and the limitations of the school timetable. Instead, the students felt blamed, and the teaching staff assumed things were declining because they couldn't get through all the curriculum material. Moreover, because the school repeated this ritual daily, the school community tolerated the intolerable. Systems of harm can thus be sustainable if the system's energy, organisational blindness and the normalisation of such rituals of the school community become tolerant to the harm that allows the system to maintain these experiences. This explains how, when marginalised groups complain about key issues, no action is taken: because the harm does not get articulated as a system issue. Therefore, school leaders must recognise two things: (*a*) when the *system* is causing harm and enabling its recurrence and (*b*) that the system's behaviour is not dependent on any single system feature. A system's behaviour derives from interactions between its components, not the components themselves. As mentioned earlier, the biggest challenges in school leadership require leaders to recognise when a system perpetuates interactions in which everyone complies with expectations to the overall detriment of the school community. Indeed, only by recognising a complex system's features can its harms be identified and changed. The important point to make is that social systems do not have a moral imperative to be humane; they can be developed to cause harm by design or drift away from the ideals of those in the system to organically become more harmful. This leads to another aspect of sustaining school systems for leaders, which are the stories told about the system.

8.3 System leaders and organisational narratives

When dealing with socially complex systems such as schools, leaders must recognise the power of the narrative, that is, the story that is told about the school. Grabbing attention and communicating key information, a narrative can come at a cost – and can cost a lot to change. If you consider your school, what story is being told? Collective narratives are inextricably bound up with a school's connections and relationships (or lack thereof). It is crucial for systems leaders to understand different types of system narratives. As we have said, history matters in systems, as do the perceived boundaries. Organisational narrative connects both history and perceived boundaries in social systems. I became fascinated with this issue while working in schools and built an accompanying typology (see Figure 8.2 below) that includes the following narratives I have identified:

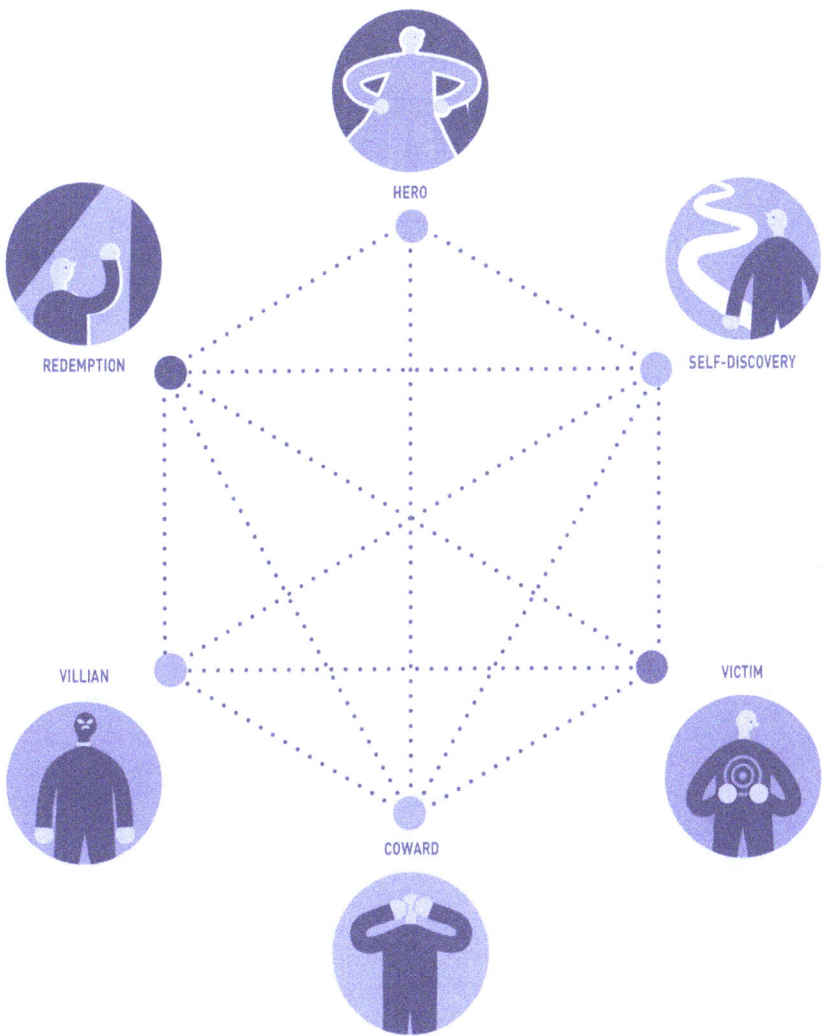

Figure 8.2 Types of organisational narrative.

1. **The hero narrative** is based on the belief that a problem or challenge needs addressing and can be overcome. Hence, system leaders mobilize the collective endeavor of the community to overcome the challenge.
2. **The journey of self-discovery** recognises that some things are unknown; thus, the school community and system leaders must go on a journey to understand themselves and what they could be become.
3. **The victim narrative** assumes that little can be done; a situation is causing harm, but the individual, group or school community affected feels too disempowered to address it. Consequently, the harm – and lack of solutions – is repeatedly discussed. In this narrative, collective trauma is often accompanied by an inability to be present- or future-orientated.
4. **The villain narrative** means members cause harm, justifying it to an end. No one likes to be associated with this narrative or identifies with it, but this can be closely linked with the perpetuation of systems of harm.
5. **The coward narrative** is where leaders fail to address a system issue. This can be avoiding the issues such as using the language of risk and uncertainty to slow or stop things for fear of a personal or reputational loss, which has a system consequence. There is also likely to be an acts of omission; no decision is a decision, so that the status quo is maintained, which affirms existing positions in the systems. Again, no one seems to like be associated with this narrative.
6. **The redemption narrative** is where school leaders or community members recognise that they have caused harm or distress and seek to make things right and move on from their mistakes by improving the system for the benefit of the school community.

Importantly, because socially complex adaptive systems are adaptive, one type of organisational narrative can turn into any other. The hero leadership team able to turn the school around can become addicted to the moment of triumph, refusing to change as new challenges emerge. Over time, they adopt the victim narrative, perceiving that things just don't seem to go their way, and there's nothing they can do about it.

Narrative boundaries are important: how different components of the school community perceive the story matters. While a leadership team may perceive themselves as heroic, their staff may perceive them as cowardly, failing to address the issues of concern to them. Similarly, students may perceive the leadership team as villainous, imposing Draconian rules that undermine their trust that the team has their best interests at heart (rather than, for example, the school's reputation). This classic issue occurs when new leaders seek to be the heroes of order, usually resulting in stringent rule enforcement on the first day of school, capturing media attention because students are sent home for failing to wear the correct uniform.

Therefore, systems leaders must recognise how important narrative is to *both* implementation and sustainability. Helping a school community shift its organisational narrative to tell a different story depends on understanding how to (*a*) amplify the new narrative through the system's networks, (*b*) supply it with systems energy and (*c*) link it with the future system state. Having been in schools struggling with low morale, I know it is not the statistics or action plans that make a significant change but their *story*. In one school with an entrenched blame culture, the strength of the victim narrative was a powerful way of maintaining inaction, as everyone else was to blame for their predicament. The effect of this was blocking the steps required to create a joyful and positive educational experience, because of the dominance of this narrative. When the new head teacher worked with the staff to change their narrative from victim to journey of self-discovery, the network effect began to shift the narrative. While the staff perceived this as for the students, the new head teacher encouraged staff to nurture and support each other as part of supporting the students, the evidence for the narrative shift started to emerge in the interactions. The school embodied this narrative over time, to the point where when you visited, staff hugged and greeted each other and to my surprise hugging me even though I was an external partner, creating an authentic sense of care for anyone on the school grounds.[11] This story amplified and shifted parental and local authority narratives about what it meant to be at that school. Therefore, systems leaders seeking to sustain school change need to blend the organisational narrative with the change they seek, recognising that both the actual change and the story of change may need to evolve to remain relevant and relatable to all members of the school community. As the narrative shifts, amplifying and regulating the story being told in the school community is fundamental to sustaining the changes systems leaders wish to see. We will therefore look at system indicators next which help to provide evidence to organizational narratives.

8.4 System indicators

How do we know whether a system is changing? School leaders often seek to measure change via before-and-after measures or outcomes and outputs. A student once asked me, "How do you measure a system?" I responded by asking, "How do you measure the health of a forest?"[12] Part of developing systems indicators is understanding interdependence and interconnection. As systems indicators cross boundaries, the focus is on the relationship *between* rather than the relationship *within*. The reductionism of systems happens when targets are created that measure only an aspect of the system. The target measures what is happening *within* a component – for example, how many students sign up for a club. What is fails to do is tell system leaders how many students interact with all clubs in a school or other provisions, such as what is the membership of students *between* all the clubs in the school. Targets do not tell system leaders what is the level of interconnectedness, that is, the healthiness of all clubs to the school community. Targets, audits and inspection frameworks often deconstruct schools yet expect the school community to be greater than the parts being assessed. This may be useful for a complicated system, but not a complex adaptive system such as a school. Systems indicators, therefore, use features such as system amplification and regulation, weighted interaction and network shapes to help understand which system features are sustainable and which have fragility. This raises the question for system leaders as to what the indicators are signally at a system level and how they respond.

The key aspect of system indicators is ensuring that they are goal-orientated rather than avoidance-driven. A system leader is tempted to assume a directly causal relationship between reducing a 'problem' and increasing the system's efficiency, that is, to assume that a reduction in X leads to an improvement in Y. The cognitive trap of avoidance-driven indicators lies partly in terms like 'defensible decision-making', which drives an underlying assumption that we need to justify what's gone wrong rather than recognise what's changed for the better. When developing system indicators, systems leaders must have an explicit goal at the beginning so that systems energy can be directed towards achieving goal-oriented activities, which will be signalled by the indicators. For this reason, a system statement and future organisational metaphor help systems leaders and stakeholders identify the most appropriate indicators of change.

To identify appropriate systems indicators, leaders must engage with stakeholders to discover which system aspects they perceive as changing over time. Participation in system indicators helps generate discussion on "How do we know when things start to change?" Moreover, drawing on stakeholders' collective knowledge helps (*a*) systems leaders understand what matters most to them, and (*b*) stakeholders feel included in the systems change because their voice has been heard. By co-constructing systems indicators, system leaders gain a shared understanding of what matters to stakeholders and how change might look like for them within the system. This can be very different from what system leaders expect. Once when I was helping a primary school review its behaviour policy, the students were asked what would improve behaviour? They responded, kindness. When this was explored further, I was clear that the discussion on improving school behaviour and discipline was avoidance motivated in terms that the concern was that behaviour could get worse. Whereas, with kindness, both staff and students agreed that in the school community they wanted to amplify this as much as possible. The school changed the policy to the school kindness policy, and consulted on what kindness meant for everyone and how could they know it was happening during the school day. For me it was an early example of developing system indicators in an inclusive way to maximise communication and participation.

For system leaders, co-constructing indicators of change over time would also be needed to reach that future vision. As mentioned above, one system indicator would be a shift in narrative, for example, from a journey of self-discovery to a hero narrative, as the school overcomes a particular challenge. Capturing the signals in terms of system energy is a way to show how attention, information and money may now be flowing to different parts of the system.

The primary question in developing systems indicators is 'how?' How did we know the system before? How do we know the system now? How could we know the system in the future? Posing 'how' questions enables systems leaders to link an indicator to a change in systems behaviour. When working with stakeholder networks, systems indicators can thus be a source of creativity, potentially forming part of the solution regarding the system's ability to self-recognise its potential for change or metamorphosis. Furthermore, finding ways to recognise changes in the system can be a collaborative experience that enables stakeholders to self-reflect on what matters most to them.

System indicators are crucial to the sustainability of systems change in schools, not just because of what they indicate but because of what attention to them represents: that a school community is still investing social energy in measuring the success of a systems change. Thus, system indicators are a way of embedding memories and reminders into school; the more creative and emotionally engaging they are, the more likely their retention in the system. Preferably, system indicators re-enforce and amplify the organisational narrative system leaders seek for the school. For example, suppose school leaders seek to change their system to promote dyslexic students' sense of belonging. In that case, their goal links with a 'journey of self-discovery' narrative, that is, being open in recognising that they may not know what that cohort of students' lived experience is and what pedagogical changes are required. Developing systems indicators would involve working not just with dyslexic students but also with other students who may have recognised times they themselves struggled and did not know what to do. One possible system indicator could be non-dyslexic students identifying opportunities to offer appropriate help. In addition, by understanding how they could offer support, they create the system leaders' desired change: improving the sense of belonging in the school. The final point is that no single indicator can tell the whole story of systems change; instead, the systems leader's goal is to develop multiple indicators that track the experience of change from different stakeholder perspectives. In this way, interdependency and interconnection are explicit in understanding how the system behaves now and in the future.

8.5 Summary

The chapter has explored models of school change and offered a critique of why system leaders need to be mindful of the school change model they use. As we have seen, the most fragile school change is with the individual – the myth of the hero-innovator. Yet there is a seductive aspect to having a charismatic individual come along and say, "I know all the answers to this school's problems, and I can do it". Therefore, system leaders need to be on-guard to individuals claiming they can be the change agents. This equates to competent leadership, which will not bring about a sustainable change in the school. Similarly, the critique of the whole-school approach has indicated that although there may be merits to this change model as a form of implementation, it has a low success rate in providing sustained change. What's more, it risks providing a veneer that change is occurring without addressing the underlying dynamics of the school as a system. System leaders need to be able to think beyond the implementation point and ask questions that require a recognition of local creativity and the ability of all members of the school community to participate. Pockets of practice may be more sustainable than either the hero-innovator or whole-school approach, but they do not require system leaders to think big or differently regarding the changes they wish to see in there school. Indeed, a pocket of practice may become a pocket of resistance to the changes they wish to make, returning to Rogers' diffusion of innovation: what was once pioneering becomes a laggard. Finally, we have explored the use of complex adaptive systems to address longer-term change. Recognition of the eco-system is essential, and the socially complexity of school must be sensitive to wider changes to survive, thrive or die.

There has also been a caution that in socially complex system in education may sustain systems of harm and instigate a pattern which harms individuals or groups of the school community itself. For system leaders, the ability for emergence means recognising not just when something new and beneficial emerges but also when such emergence causes harm. The ability of harmful systems to sustain themselves is in part due to the normalisation that hides the harm occurring i.e., tolerance of the intolerable. System leaders using empowering participatory means will be more sensitive to early signals this is occurring.

Recognizing signals of harm or success is a crucial skill for system leaders to develop and understand the narratives in their settings. Educational settings are socially complex. Storytelling enables members of the school community to link the past to the present. Furthermore, it identifies where others are positioned between consensus and discord in comparison to our own position and perspectives. Organisational narrative is an excellent indicator of change in the system. As such, system leaders must be skilled balancing the opportunities of the school's existing narrative with the ability for a new one to emerge, which enables the school to adapt to what could be achieved in their future system statement.

Finally, we have identified system indicators as a means of articulating and recognising interconnection and interdependence. System indicators provide evidence for the organisational narrative not only that change is occurring but that the school community has participated in the shift. For system leaders, indicators of the change are not a product but rather an ongoing process of adaptation. They enable the ongoing story of how the present arrives at the future. They are essential to demonstrating how the system learnt over time and still does.

In Chapter 9, we will conclude with reflections on what this means for system leaders within the educational eco-system.

Notes

1 The fruits of which you are now reading.
2 Using a complexity approach of feedback, network shapes, boundaries, time and opportunities for emergence.
3 There may be the possibility of new network share emerging, depending on weight of interaction and feedback in the system.

4 We return to the point about pilots and projects, which become a pocket of practice over time but do affect the overarching system.
 5 This is not to say the function is not important to the system, but rather there is a loss in interconnection, and a failure to recognise interdependence.
 6 In one school they paid huge sums to a behaviour consultant to come in, and as far as I could see delivered nothing, yet they were delighted to be working with him as he had a national reputation!
 7 *Implementation of Whole School Restorative Approaches to Promote Positive Youth Development: Review of Relevant Literature and Practice Guidelines* (2022)
 8 Youth Justice Board for England and Wales.
 9 The stance of the school was that this was an issue for parents as they bought the devices and was beyond the school. The physical boundary was the mental boundary as well!
10 This does not just mean money, but also information and attention.
11 There was a lot more being done in the school such as eating together and understanding the psychological importance of nurture and attachment. But it was also the hugs I remember.
12 This led to a really great discussion on interconnection, diversity and sustainability.

9 Conclusions on thinking big and thinking differently

This book aimed to introduce educationalists and those interested in educational change to systems-thinking ideas, particularly a complexity approach to school change. We have considered different system types – simple, complicated, chaotic and complex – to help you recognise what kind is involved when there are calls to 'change the system'. I have focused on a complexity approach as a lens for the realities of school change. Although no theory can accurately model every nuance of reality, I believe that the complexity approach enables systems leaders to better recognise the scale and opportunities of the challenge they face. Furthermore, a complexity approach answers many concerns inherent in calling for change whilst avoiding the pitfalls other models' changes have to the detriment of the school community. A complexity approach provides system leaders with a conceptual framework for 'play' – and I do not use 'play' flippantly here. Rather, I use it to emphasise how important play is as a dynamic learning process that helps leaders feel safe exploring boundaries, making mistakes and understanding their system's rules. This echoes Cilliers' work:

> When dealing with complex phenomena, no single method will yield the whole truth.
>
> Approaching a complex system playfully allows for different avenues of advance, different viewpoints, and, perhaps, a better understanding of its characteristics.
>
> (Cilliers, 1998, p. 23)

Therefore, we must delight in our discoveries and enjoy our experiences of working in complex systems. For system leaders, thinking big and thinking differently requires a playful mindset in which to engage their system of interest.

9.1 The fallacy of experience

One aspect of becoming a system leader is relinquishing the medal of experience. Leaders often impress upon me that they have 10, 25 or 50 years of experience. However, such experience tells them only what's worked in the *past*. While experience may help leaders to recognise patterns and build cognitive simulations of likely trajectories, the school environment's stability creates a personal perspective of familiarity that professionals qualify as 'experience'. However, such experience may *hinder* system change, causing leaders to focus on similarities with their previous experience rather than recognising the new and unique eco-system they face. Familiarity can inhibit creativity since it feels easier and safer to rely on tried-and-tested approaches rather than explore something new and unknown. Therefore, experience is not an indicator of a person's ability to navigate a new system and may even predispose leaders towards overconfidence that they understand their school from a privileged point of knowing. Therefore, they risk validating their decisions based on previous successes, rather than seeking to playfully engage with possibility. If we return to the production-line metaphor, someone who was able to maintain a machine for 20 years does not necessarily know how to create a new product or experience. And unlike a production line, education requires constant adaptation. Yet educational management theory – and, by extension, school leadership – sends mixed messages by championing school leaders while valuing only their experience, which perpetuates the myth of the hero-innovator.

A complexity approach considers the totality of a system's interactions, and the complexity framework developed over the course of this book is critical for thinking differently. While school leaders may intuitively 'sense' system features or changes, the legacy of production-line management predisposes them toward 'fixing' the supposed fault rather than exploring whether the whole machine is working as intended. Interestingly, the COVID-19 experience changed the entire education system: schools and educational settings went from classrooms of millions to millions of classrooms. Leaders could not draw on previous pandemic experiences; instead, they needed to be willing to listen to cross-sector advice – for example, medical experts – as well as the school community. This included understanding how amplification affected the school community's health, organising new network shapes to include parents and carers in the learning experience[1] and finding emergent ways to keep relationships going in a COVID-19-safe way and ensuring safe boundaries for learning. In effect, all stakeholders temporarily became systems leaders.

The production-line approach of Taylorism values the standardisation and regularity that would have been vital for the industrial era. However, alongside the COVID-19 pandemic, societal, work and technological changes meant standardisation and regularity no longer reflected school communities' needs. Instead, I have put forward that systems leaders prepare school communities to recognise the value of different perspectives, empathise with other members and their decisions, and recognise the importance of co-designing and envisaging shared futures. This is why I believe thinking in systems is vital. It is not enough to apply interventions or initiatives like sticking plasters; recognising how we think about schools and their place in communities requires a paradigm shift from production-line to eco-system thinking. Hence, thinking big means changing the lens systems leaders use to identify and understand their schools' problems and challenges.

9.2 Creativity and evolution

When considering systems change, I have typically used four phases of change to reflect the state of change intention: implementation, embedding, innovating and sustaining. I explored implementation extensively in Chapter 7, while in Chapter 8, I addressed the mindset shift to embedding and ultimately sustaining the changes in educational settings. However, local creativity often emerges in the innovation phase. Through new opportunities to meet and connect, systems leaders can facilitate opportunities to create solutions. For those engaged in the change, this is when new connections emerge or previous boundaries disappear.

However, innovation can be momentary, without sustainability. Schools can be highly innovative places – indeed, learning depends on finding and sustaining new connections – but we must now apply this to *system learning*. The knowledge system leaders need is available in the system's interactions, collective narrative and member experiences. By creating appropriate system indicators, system leaders allow the system to self-regulate its progress from implementation to sustainability. Furthermore, collaboration with different stakeholders' system indicators enables the school community and system leaders to recognise whether the system is surviving, thriving or declining.

The complexity approach helps ensure good things aren't lost by being personality-led or niche-bound. The four phases – implementing, embedding, innovating and sustaining – are not time-bound; they are phases of development, and the transitions to implement a change, and other phases may be shorter or longer, relative to the system's ability to adapt. This is because each stage is relative to other things happening in the school. The system leader must decide how to progress at each phase based on the school community's needs and the system's pushback.

If I were to add a phase, I think it would be *decline*. Systems have finite energy and need new sources to replenish them. The complexity approach focuses on ensuring change survives or thrives in the school community. However, systems leaders make decisions about the system's survival. When a change initiative loses systems energy, it can deteriorate until it no longer retains attention, information or monetary resources. Alternatively, change can come to an abrupt halt if the system energy sustaining it discontinues, which is often the case with school pilots: when the funds cease, so too does attention and information.

As Chapter 4 emphasised that no feedback is a form of feedback, often suggesting that a system feature is no longer relevant to the system's needs. While expiration is a natural part of systems change, leaders can overcome it through adaptation. As Chapter 4 mentioned, changing a network's shape prevents an overreliance on the hub. For example, turning a hub-and-spoke network into a loose or meshed network increases information retention within the system, while overreliance on a single leader renders a system-change's lifespan too dependent on that person. Likewise, network shapes can exist for longer than their purpose, for example, the hub-and-spoke network retains centralised resources even when the spokes are mature enough to connect in alternative ways. Similarly, outdated or redundant systems' artefacts create organizational noise that distracts or depletes attention.

Thus, the causes of school decline are rarely due to one big event but rather a continuous failure to understand the school's system dynamics and organisational blindness about what is perpetuating the decline. In such cases, silos seek to protect their part of the system whilst failing to recognise the school's overarching deterioration. System leaders must recognise when the *system* – rather than its components – is failing and what this means for the school community and its wider local community. Systems leaders also need to recognise the impermanence of change, understanding that it is not an end state even when system indicators are achieved.

9.3 Systems of learning

The sense of education repeating itself rather than evolving to meet society's needs is not just because of leaders' short-termism or schools' performance-driven cultures. A more fundamental issue is that the very institutions designed to promote learning no longer learn themselves, and the loss of organisational memory costs schools as complex adaptive systems. A school's history matters, and the school community's ability to recognise what has gone before avoids reinventing the wheel. Importantly, remembering the school's successes is just as important; there is a tendency to remember when things did not work rather than when they do. However, such memories are lost in the production-line focus on continuous improvement, where there is no time to look back and celebrate what the school achieved as a community or to say, "This is what matters to us because we were there". While a school's culture is a memory repository, it is not an entirely accurate one; instead, it is prone to gaps and myths. System leaders seeking to sustain change in their schools must create a collective memory for members to revisit, reminding them of what it is and why it matters.

Thus, it is vital to curate the school's organisational narrative and develop systems artefacts. If the collective memory becomes cluttered with organisational noise, it becomes obscured and likely forgotten. Systems leaders must curate the organisational narrative to ensure the accessibility of success memories to inform the present and enable the future. The fatigue many schools face in organisational change may not necessarily be because of the change itself, but because the process has become a never-ending treadmill, or the equivalent of each time schools metaphorically climb one mountain, they immediately face the next, ultimately forgetting the 'why' in the constant activity of 'when' and 'how' to overcome the next challenge, term or year. This is where systems leaders can playfully explore the present and future states of their system: This is where systems leaders can harness the interconnection and interdependency of narratives, networks and interaction weights to enable the school to become a learning system. Hence, the ultimate end is nurturing a system towards self-management so that it can evolve *without* them.

9.4 Beyond the system leader

Above all, systems leaders must recognise their impermanence in the system. They must create networks that can sustain change and recognise that the change they fostered will continue beyond them. System leaders must also ensure their system can survive independently of prominent personalities or charismatic leaders. Seen through the production-line lens, leaders who leave the system are simply a lost cog in the mechanics, replaceable without a loss of production. In contrast, the loss of a systems leader from the complex adaptive system of a school means a loss of knowledge and connection. Therefore, it is incumbent upon systems leaders to consider how connections and interdependencies can be maintained once they have left the system, setting up a sustainable learning system that does not depend on them. Rather than leaving a legacy of reputation, systems leaders must therefore leave a legacy of *change* that enables a school and its community to have confidence in an envisioned future and equips them with a system that can adapt and identify its own indicators for success. To do so means letting go of ownership, thus empowering continued evolution in the future. This may be the ultimate sign of sustainability, since what matters most is never the responsibility of a single individual but of the collective school community.

9.5 A complexity approach to thinking big and thinking differently

A complexity approach is about *application*, enabling systems leaders to engage with the system and implement change. My lack of knowledge about systems early in my career meant I replicated many of the same problems I now seek to address. My biggest frustration lay in the intervention/initiative successes that deteriorated to the detriment of a school community; the failure to sustain change means that schools serving communities already suffering from inequality and deprivation continue perpetuating it. This is why I so vehemently oppose the 'quick wins' or 'low-hanging fruit' promoted by management jargon – these equate to tokenistic and futile strategies in complex adaptive systems.

Although external information may occasionally be required, schools have unwittingly helped create an industry of consultants and guest speakers who inform the school community but do not change their experiences. This ritual plays out at the start of every school year with schools continuing to pay for external expertise rather than create and connect new knowledge. Moreover, there is the risk it creates a disposable information model, as PowerPoint slides and handouts change little beyond the INSET when viewed as a niche.[2] External information, when viewed as a cross-boundary way of knowing, enables system leaders to bring new sources of system energy in rather a yearly recommissioning ritual. Furthermore, by externalising information, and thus creativity, in the form of an expert, schools become over-reliant on others providing new insights rather than genuinely and authentically engaging their communities' creativity and learning. The tendency to bring in external speakers allows the dominant system to continue unchanged, creating subservient systems bound by the narrative of doing something for a specific group in the school. However, this outsourcing of creativity runs the risk of ignoring the importance of the system to learn and accommodate new forms of knowledge. Systems leaders must filter out the best external knowledge, identifying what enhances their system's resilience and fitness and supports the desired change.

Attempting to change individuals may offer short-term benefits – possibly boosting reputational status – but does not fundamentally change the underlying system problem. Although thinking big and thinking differently can be challenging without a cognitive springboard, the complexity approach framework helps leaders apply system-change ideas. Transitioning from implementation to embedding means going from amplifying to regulating social energy in the system. Likewise, sensitivity to system change means recognising that organic and intentional emergence indicates a system shift from embedding to innovation. Finally, sustainability requires systems leaders to let go and see how the system behaves when they no longer lead school change.

9.6 Final reflections

The dominant legacy of the production-line approach has meant that, even whilst writing this book, I have had to constantly self-regulate my language to protect against its gravitational pull. Systems thinking is a subservient system, and the complexity approach is a sub-system of a subservient school leadership system. Therefore, it is susceptible to dominant mechanistic leadership thinking. During my PhD, I realised that however much work the schools who engaged me did towards systems change, they could still end up with a RAG-rated action with plan. I realised at this point that this was the system maintaining itself through expected performance norms and language rituals. Thus, systems indicators are vital to prevent falling back into the trap of mechanistic leadership, and I have chosen language throughout this book to remind me to always 'think system'.

On this note, I'd like to offer three key take-home messages to help you on your journey:

1. **THINK SYSTEM**: Prevailing management theories will always try to pull you back into component, cause-and-effect and mechanistic thinking, and

it's taken me years to develop resistance to this prevailing narrative and unlearn the unhelpful programming. To counter this requires active commitment. Whatever the problem appears to be, *think system*.
2. **THINK CREATIVITY**: If you *think system*, you'll see and naturally enable creativity to emerge. By *thinking in system*, you unlock creative potential – not just in yourself but your networks and give permission for others to share their perspectives and creativity.
3. **THINK SUSTAINABILITY**: Build bridges from what could be the future and how you would enable those who come after us to build their own. The role of the systems leader is to co-ordinate and empower the school community to realise its emergent potential, which enables everyone to participate in sharing the future.

Notes

1. At the time, I became daddy teacher help to keep my then five-year-old daughter engaged in screen time with her teachers.
2. I was in a school, discussing with a group of staff how their year was going; they shared that they had recently enjoyed an INSET, but did not see how it related to their everyday role or the range of other initiatives happening in the school.

References

Arnstien, S. (1969). A ladder of citizen participation, *Journal of the American Planning Association* vol: 35, no. 4, pp. 216–224. DOI: 10.1080/01944366908977225

Bonell, C., Allen, E., Warren, E., McGowan, J., Bevilacqua, L., Jamal, F., Legood, R., Wiggins, M., Opondo, C., Mathiot, A., Sturgess, J., Fletcher, A., Sadique, Z., Elbourne, D.,Christie, D., Bond, L., Scott, S., and Viner, R. M. (2018). Effects of the learning together intervention on bullying and aggression in English secondary schools (INCLUSIVE): a cluster randomised controlled trial. *Lancet* vol: 392, pp. 2452–2464.

Byrne, D., and Callaghan, G. (2014). *Complexity Theory and The Social Sciences: The State of the Art*. Routledge.

Chabris, C, and Simons, D. (2011). *The Invisible Gorilla*. Broadway Paperbacks.

Checkland, P., and Scholes, J. (1999). *Soft Systems Methodology in Action*. Wiley.

Cilliers, P. (1998). *Complexity and Postmodernism: Understanding Complex Systems*. Routledge.

Cowie, H. (2013). Restorative practice in school: a psychological perspective. In Sellman, E., Cremin, H., and McCluskey, G (Eds) *Restorative Approaches to Conflict in Schools: International Perspectives on Managing Relationships in the Classroom*. London: Routledge.

Cremin, H. (2019). *Masquerading System*. Personal Correspondence 9th May 2019.

Davenport, T. H., and Beck, J. C. (2001). *The Attention Economy: Understanding the New Currency of Business*. Harvard Business School Press.

Davies, L. (2004). *Education and Conflict: Complexity and Chaos*. Routledge.

Davis, B., and Sumara, D. (2006). *Complexity and Education: Inquiries into Learning, Teaching, and Research*. Lawrence Erlbaum Associates. Taylor & Francis Group.

Desautels, L. L. (2020). *Connections over Compliance: Rewiring Our Perceptions of Discipline*. Revelations in Education.

Ekma, P. (2003). *Emotions Revealed: Understanding Faces and Feelings*. A Phoenix Paperback.

Ekman, P., and Wallace, V. F. (2003). *Unmasking The Face: A Guide to Recognising Emotions and Facial Expressions*. Major Books.

Freire, P. (1970). *Pedagogy of the Oppressed*. 30th Anniversary Edition. New York: Continuum.

Georgiades, N., and Phillimore, L. (1975). The myth of the Hero-Innovator and alternative strategies for organisational change. In Kiernan, C. C., and Woodford, P. F. (Eds) *Behaviour Modification with Severely Retarded: Study Group 8 of the Institute for Research into Mental and Multiple Handicap.* Elsevier, Associated Scientific Publishers.

Hargreaves, A. and Fink, D. (2006). *Sustainable Leadership.* Jossey-Bass. A Wiley Imprint.

Hebb, D. O. (1949). *The Organisation of Behaviour: A Neuropshycological Theory.* John Wiley and Sons Inc.

Kahneman, D., Sibony, O., and Sunstein, C. R. (2021). *Noise: A Flaw in Human Judgement.* William Collins.

Katz, D., and Kahn, R. L. (1966). *The Social Psychology of Organisations.* New York: Wiley.

Lorenz, E. (1972). Predictability: does the flap of a butterfly's wings in Brazil set off a tornado in Texas? *American Association for the Advancement of Sciences; 139th meeting.*

Mahon, A., Clarke, D. F., and Hunt, A. R. (2018). The role of attention in eye movement awareness. *Attention, Perception and Psychophysics* vol: 80, pp. 1691–1704.

Mas-Expósito, L., Krieger, V., Amador-Campos, J.A., Casañas, R., Albertí, M., and Lalucat-Jo, L. (2022). Implementation of whole school restorative approaches to promote positive youth development: review of relevant literature and practice guidelines. *Education Sciences* vol: 12, p. 187. DOI: 10.3390/educsci12030187

Mason, M. (Eds) (2008). *Complexity Theory and Educational Philosophy.* Wiley-Blackwell. A John Wiley and Sons Publication.

Meadows, D., Meadows, L., Randers, J., and Behrens III, W. W. (1972). *The Limits of Growth.* Potomac Associates, Universe Books.

Meadows, D. H. (2008). *Thinking in Systems: A Primer*, Wright, D. (Ed). Chelsea Green Publishing.

Miles, M. B. (Ed) (1964). *Innovation in Education.* Teachers College, New York.

Miller, G. A. (1956). The magical number seven, plus or minus two: some limits on our capacity for processing information. *Psychological Review* vol: 63, no. 2, pp. 81–97.

Nonaka, I., and Takeuchi, H. (1995). Organisational knowledge creation. Extract from the knowledge creating company. Reprinted in Henry, J. (2006). *Creative Management and Development.* (3rd Ed)., pp. 64–81. Open University.

Osberg, D., Biesta, G., & Cilliers, P., (2008). From representation to emergence: complexity's challenge to the epistemology of schooling, *Educational Philosophy and Theory*, vol: 40, no. 1, pp. 213–227. DOI: 10.1111/j.1469-5812.2007.00407.x

Roberts, L. (2013). *Restorative Approaches: A Sustainable Whole School Approach?* Masters in Educational Research. University of Cambridge.

Roberts, L. (2020). *Bullying in Schools: A Complexity Approach to Sustainable Resotrative Apporaches?* Faculty of Education, Cambridge University. DOI: 10.17863/CAM.56573

Rogers, E. M. (2003). *Diffusion of Innovation.* 5th Edition. Free Press.

Rose, T. (2015). *The End of Average: How to Succeed in a World that Values Sameness.* Penguin Books.

Sellman, E., Cremin, H., and McCluskey, G. (Eds) (2013). *Restorative Approaches to Conflict in Schools: International Perspectives on Managing Relationships in the Classroom.* Routledge.

Skinns, L., Du Rose, N., and Hough, M. (2009). *An Evaluation of Bristol RAiS.* King's College.

Taylor, F. W. (1919). *The Principles of Scientific Management.* Harper and Brothers Publishers.

Thompson, P. (2010). *Whole School Change: A Literature Review*. (2nd Ed). Creativity, Culture and Education.

UK Parliament, Writtin questions, answers and statements. (2021). Youth Custody: Costs. https://questions-statements.parliament.uk/written-questions/detail/2021-07-14/33308 cost of placement in youth custody.

van der Kolk, B. A. (2014). *The Body Keeps the Score: Brain, Mind, and Body in the Healing of Trauma*. Viking.

Wong, D. S. W., Cheng, C. H. K., Ngan, R. M. H., and Ma, S. K. (2010). Program effectiveness of a restorative whole-school approach to tackling bullying in Hong Kong. *International Journal of therapy and Comparative Criminology* vol: 55, no. 6, pp. 846–862. DOI: 10.1177/0306624X10374638

Youth Justice Board. (2005). *Restorative Justice in Schools*. Youth Justice Board.

YouGov (2019). Exploring the issue of off-rolling, on behalf of Ofsted. www.gov.uk: https://www.gov.uk/government/publications/off-rolling-exploring-the-issue#:~:text=Details,best%20interests%20of%20the%20pupil.

Index

Pages in *italics* refer to figures, pages in **bold** refer to tables, and pages followed by "n" refer to notes.

academic journey 1–3; English educational system 3–5; gap between theory and practice in schools 5–6
Ackoff, Russell 92
adverse childhood experiences (ACEs) 87, 93n7
American Industrialisation 10
amplification 31–32
Arnstien, S. **69**, 69–74, 77n2–77n3
Ashe, Arthur 78
attention: attentional redundancy 54; definition 47–48; emotions 51–52; organisational concentration 49–50; organisational focus 48–49; organisational noise 52–53

Barrow, Dame Jocelyn 3, 9n1
Booth, Tony 5–6
boundaries 41–43
Butterfly Effect 22–23, *22*
Byrne, D. 28

Callaghan, G. 28
Chaos Theory 21–23
Chaotic system: Butterfly Effect 22–23, *22*; Chaos Theory 22; fractal structure 23; system lock-in 24–25; unpredictable regularity 24
charismatic leaders 136
Checkland, P. 74, 100, 102
Cilliers, P. 132
Clapham Common communities 3
closed system 41
cognitive trap 88–89
complex adaptive systems (CASs) 121–122; amplification 31–32; boundaries 41–43; complexity theory 27–30; computer simulations 27; emergence *39*, 39–40; feedback 30; Hebb's Rule 33–35; hub-and-spoke network 35–36; interconnection 26; interdependency 26–27; loose network 37–38; network of networks 38–39; network shapes *36*; regulatory feedback 32–33; scale of 27; time 43–45, *44*
Complexity Theory 1; as multi-disciplinary science 27–28; in natural and mathematical sciences 28–30; positive and negative feedback 30
complicated systems 18–21, *19*
component thinking 10–15
computer simulations 27
COVID-19 pandemic 37, 133
Craig 77n4
Cremin, H. 2–3, 76, 114
Croydon Council 5
curriculum-driven learning 12

Davis, B. 35
Department for Education (DfE) 57
diffusion of innovation model 90, *91*, 119, 130
dominant legacy 137–138
Du Rose, N. 116

education: complexity of 15; component management in 20; and educational research 29; negative fractal patterns in 25; primary and secondary 1; results-oriented 15; socially complex system in 130; as a societal production line 11–13; system's history 15; in the UK 81
educational policies 11

educational sustainability 112–113
education system's history 15
Ekman, P. 52, 60n3
England's educational marketisation 6
English educational system 3–5, 12

feedback 30
Fink, D. 112
Freire, P. 77n1

General Certificate of Education (GCSEs) 13
Georgiades, N. 78, 93n1, 115–116

Hargreaves, A. 112
Hasselmann, Klaus 28
Hebb, D. O. 33–35
Hebb's Rule 33–35
Hill, Dawn 3
Hough, M. 116
hub-and-spoke network 35–36

information: definition 54; explicit information 54–55; implicit information 55–56
In Service Education and Training (INSET) 38, 44
In-Service Education Training (INSET) 20, 57–59, 80, 119, 122, 137, 138n2
intuitive system leadership 80

Jensen 56

Kahneman, D. 53
Kahn, R. L. 115
Katz, D. 115
Klein, Gary 80

Lambeth Local Education Authority 2
language 55, 67, 75–77, 87, 97, 101, 110, 119, 126, 137
League Tables 12–15, 68, 82
The Limits of Growth 112
loose network 37–38
Lorenz, E. 21–22

Manabe, Syukuro 28
Meadows, D. 12, 14
meshed network 35, 37–38, 59, 62, 135
money: conversion into system resources 57–59; as energy 56–57
multicultural tensions 4
the myth of the hero-innovator 78–79, 115–116

negative feedback *see* regulatory feedback
network of networks 38–39
network shapes 35–40, *36*, 44, 65–66, 70, 72, 74, 86, 94, 106, 116, 121, 127, 133, 135
Newtonian clockwork-universe metaphor 103
Nonaka, I. 54

open system 41
organisational narratives 124–127, *125*, 129–130, 135

parents 6, 13, 17, 19–20, 22–23, 25, 31, 40, 48, 58, 64–68, 70, 73–74, 85–86, 89, 96, 104, 108, 119, 121, 133
Parisi, Giorgio 28
participation ladder 69–75
Perkins 77n4
Phillimore, L. 78, 93n1, 115–116
pockets of practice 116–118
positionality: definition 61; network position 62; position to amplify and regulate 62; power to attract 63; power to maintain 63–64; power to opt-out 64; power to reject 64; role position 61–62
positive feedback *see* amplification
power of Taylorism 51
The Principles of Scientific Management 10, 81
production-line approach 12–13, 83, 133, 137
production-line management theory 12
Pupil Referral Units (PRUs) 80, 85

racism 5, 49, 66, 109
Red, Amber, Green (RAG) rating system 21, 55, 76, 137
regulatory feedback 32–33
Robinson, Ken 83
Rogers, E. M. 90, *91*, 98, 111n3, 119, 130
Rose, T. 83

Scholes, J. 100, 102
school and community's history 15
school leaders 7; practice self-awareness 8
school leadership 6, 20, 40, 55, 59, 78, 83, 96, 124, 133, 137
school participation ladder: citizen control 72–73; consulting 70–71; delegated power 72; informing 70;

144 Index

manipulation 69; navigating 73–75; partnership 71–72; placation 71; therapy 70

school's stakeholders: engaging multiple stakeholders 67–68; external partners 68; parents 66; school participation ladder 69–75; staff 65–66; students 66–67; system language 75–76

self-organisation 26, 29–30, 33–35, 37, 39, 43–46, 86, 121

self-reflection 8–9

Sibony, O. 53

silo working 82–83

simple system *16*, 16–18

Skinns, L. 116

social energy 46–47, *47*; attention 47–54; information 54–56; money 56–59

socio-cultural mix 3

Soft Systems Methodology (SSM) 74, 100, 102

staff 3–6, 12–13, 17, 20–21, 23–25, 30–34, 37–38, 40, 42, 44, 46, 48–51, 58–59, 62–67, 70–74, 79–80, 83, 85–90, 92, 94–95, 97–98, 100–101, 103–105, 107–109, 112, 115–119, 122–124, 126–128

Standard Assessment Test (SAT) 13

Sumara, D. 35

Sunstein, C. R. 53

system archetypes 19–20; chaotic system 21–25; complicated systems 18–21; definition 15–16; simple system 16–18

system change 10, 27, 37, 49, 52–54, 57–60, 64, 71, 73–77, 80, 83–86, 88, 92–111, 118–120, 123, 133, 135, 137

system language 75–76

system leaders: complex adaptive systems 135; complexity approach 133, 136–137; COVID-19 experience 37, 133; creativity and evolution 134–135; educational sustainability 112–113; engaging with stakeholders 95; future school visualisation 104; future system statement 105–106; goal-oriented system 109; implementing school change 109–110; initial mental models 96–97; legacy of change 136; medal of experience 132–133; mental map of school's system 99; models of sustainability 113–115; the myth of the hero-innovator 115–116; and organisational narratives 124–127, *125*; pockets of practice 116–118; production line model 98; rich picture 100; school metaphor 100–101, 104–105; school's ecosystem 120–123; school's history 96; school's prevailing leadership 96; senior leadership engaging 97; space and place in schools 108; stakeholders' interpretations 97; system artefacts 107–108; system change 106–107; systems indicators 127–129; systems of harm 123–124; system statement 102–103; thinking big 133–134; types of school change *114*; visualisations 101–102; whole-school approach 118–120

system leadership: cognitive trap 88–89; decision-making 80–81; framework for 79–80; intuitive 80; organisational blindness 89–90; partnerships 84; pattern recognition 81; school initiatives 85–86; school pilots 84–85; silo working 82–83; system dominance 86–88; systems pushback 90–92; Taylorism for 81–82

system lock-in 24–25

systems indicators 127–129

systems of learning 135–136

system stakeholders 65–68

Takeuchi, H. 54

Taylor, F. W. 10–11, 13, 21, 25, 81–83

Taylorism 10–11, 51, 81, 83, 88, 133

Taylorist management theory 12

Taylorist thinking 15

Taylor's scientific method 11

The Office for Standards in Education, Children's Services and Skills (Ofsted) 12–14, 69, 74, 82, 100, 103, 105, 122

think creativity 138

think sustainability 138

think system 137–138

Thompson, P. 44

time 43–45, 92

Tuckman 56

WhatsApp 37, 62

Whole School Approach (WSA) 2–3, 5, 7, 113, 115, 118–121, 129–130

For Product Safety Concerns and Information please contact our EU representative GPSR@taylorandfrancis.com
Taylor & Francis Verlag GmbH, Kaufingerstraße 24, 80331 München, Germany

www.ingramcontent.com/pod-product-compliance
Lightning Source LLC
Chambersburg PA
CBHW061718300426
44115CB00014B/2736